50 TRUE STORIES THAT WILL SCARE YOU TO DEATH

Art Director: Angela Navarra
Art Producer: Stacey Stambaugh
Editor: Kristen Depken
Production Editor: Rachel Taenzler
Production Designer: Martin Worthington

This book is based on research, interviews, and the author's interpretation of reported events. While every effort has been made to ensure accuracy, some accounts rely on personal testimony, which by its nature cannot be independently verified. Due to graphic descriptions and mature subject matter, this book is intended for mature readers and may not be suitable for all audiences.

Published by Callisto Publishing LLC C/O Sourcebooks LLC
P.O. Box 4410, Naperville, Illinois 60567-4410
(630) 961-3900
callistopublishing.com

Library of Congress Cataloging-in-Publication Data is on file with the publisher.

Printed and bound in the United States of America.
VP 10 9 8 7 6 5 4 3 2 1

50 TRUE STORIES that will SCARE you to DEATH

TRUE CRIME, HAUNTINGS, ALIENS, AND MORE

SEBASTIAN KRAHL

ILLUSTRATIONS BY FÁBIO LYRA

callisto publishing
an imprint of Sourcebooks

CONTENTS

INTRODUCTION

Hello, reader. My name is Sebastian Krahl, and for as long as I can remember, I've been drawn to the dark side of storytelling. As a kid, I was obsessed with horror movies, true crime documentaries, and anything that made my skin crawl. There was always something about creeping fear—that spine-tingling feeling of "What if this happened to me?"—that stuck with me long after the screen went dark.

As I grew up, this fascination never left. Instead, it evolved. I began creating videos about the world's most disturbing, bizarre, and terrifying true stories—real cases of evil, the unexplained, and the unimaginable. What started as a passion turned into a full-blown platform. Today, I've been telling scary stories online for over six years and have built a community of more than 9.5 million people who tune in to hear the darkest truths the world has to offer.

This book is the result of years spent delving into the unsettling corners of reality—from cold-blooded crimes to paranormal encounters and unsolved mysteries that defy logic. Every story in this book is 100 percent true. These aren't urban legends or bedtime tales meant to entertain. These are real events. Real victims. Real terror. I chose each story for a reason—whether because of how disturbing it is, how little known yet horrifying the details are, or how much it haunted me after I heard it.

You're about to read fifty of the scariest true stories I've ever come across. Some will shock you, some will disturb you, and others will stay with you long after you put this book down. Whether you're into true crime, the supernatural, alien abductions, or mysteries that can't be explained—you're in for a ride.

Turn the page if you're ready. But don't say I didn't warn you.

CHAPTER ONE

THE DEAD
Ghosts, Hauntings, and Other Paranormal Activity

THE HAUNTED HOSPITAL

TOOELE, UTAH

1953

Tooele Hospital, now infamously known as Asylum 49, is regarded as one of the most haunted buildings in the world. Also known as Utah's most notorious paranormal hot spot, Tooele Hospital has a uniquely disturbing history that has fueled its terrifying reputation. The hospital was originally constructed by a man named Samuel F. Lee, not as a medical facility, but as a private residence for his family. However, in 1913, the Lee family left, and the building was repurposed into an almshouse, sheltering those who had nowhere else to go.

As Tooele and the surrounding Utah population grew, local authorities saw potential in the structure—not as a shelter, but as a hospital. Thus, in 1953, the Tooele Hospital was officially opened. From the onset, it was plagued with severe underfunding and a lack of resources so extreme that they stacked dead bodies and stored them in an unrefrigerated room due to their lack of a proper morgue. Unsettling practices like this led many to believe the hospital should have been shut down long ago, but astonishingly, it remained open until 2001, when it was converted into a nursing home.

Currently, the original hospital operates as a haunted house attraction called Asylum 49. But during its years as a nursing home, the elderly residents who lived there were tormented by eerie, inexplicable occurrences. Among the most terrifying phenomena were the frequent sightings of ghostly children—described as small figures darting through hallways even though no children lived in the facility. These spectral figures were believed to be an omen, appearing in the home when residents were about to pass away or specifically visiting a resident who was next to die. However, paranormal experts investigating the Tooele hauntings have theorized that these so-called "children" might not have been children at all. Some researchers believe they were actually something far more sinister—possibly demons in disguise.

Beyond the phantom children, the Tooele Hospital was home to several other disturbing apparitions. One of the most well-known spirits was a ghostly nurse, always seen dressed in pure white from head to toe. This mysterious figure—known as Maria—was said to aimlessly roam the hospital's halls, but patients frequently reported being cared for by her, often describing how "the nurse in white" already helped them. This would send chills down the nurses' spines, because in reality *none* of the nurses working in the hospital wore white. Tooele's "nurse in white" was also more sinister than she appeared. It's believed she was the guardian of a portal to the afterlife. For residents who have witnessed the portal, they've described it as blindingly bright, almost otherworldly. It was believed to be a gateway through which the souls of those who died in the building passed into the next realm. Strangely, several residents reported seeing the portal a few days before their deaths, as if it was beckoning them forward.

Opposite to Maria's presence in white was the man in black, a terrifying entity that manifested at exactly 3:00 a.m.—also known as "The Devil's Hour," a time long associated with paranormal activity and demonic energy. Witnesses described him as a shadowy figure, his features hidden in darkness, yet with a presence so intimidating and oppressive that those who saw him felt an overwhelming sense of dread.

There is yet another spirit said to have haunted the hospital, the ghost of a little girl. It has been speculated that she was connected to the spectral children who visited before residents passed, but her relationship to them remains a mystery. She has mostly been witnessed by visitors of Asylum 49, who claim that this young girl follows them through the maze, appearing and disappearing at random, only to vanish without a trace before they can fully process what they've seen.

While many of the spirits that haunted the hospital were feared, not all appear to have had malicious intent. The spirit of Samuel F. Lee, who originally built Tooele Hospital as his private residence, is said to still roam the halls, watching over the building. He is accompanied by his son, Thomas, who is believed to have died when he was a young boy. Those who claim to have seen Thomas say he appears as a small boy wandering the corridors, sometimes holding his father's hand as they silently walk through the building they once called home. Uniquely, Thomas is known for his playful nature. Both visitors and staff members have reported experiencing harmless pranks—objects moving on their own, sudden light touches of a hand, and disembodied giggles echoing through the halls.

Tooele Hospital also has a strange and disturbing connection to the number three, with some even saying the building is cursed by a "rule of three." For example, when one nursing home resident would pass away, two more deaths would inevitably follow in quick succession. This pattern was so consistent that staff members came to expect and prepare for it.

There is, of course, the man in black who appeared at 3:00 a.m. and was said to be the most disturbing presence haunting Tooele Hospital. One of the most spine-chilling encounters with the man in black was when he entered a resident's room late one night and, after he was through the threshold, the door slammed shut and locked itself from the inside. Panic immediately set in, and nurses frantically called maintenance to remove the door. When they finally managed to pry it open, they rushed inside—only to find the resident had passed away. The man in black was gone, with no trace of him left behind. Some speculate that he may not have been just an entity that haunted the hospital, but something far worse—an omen of death itself.

Kimm Andersen, cocreator and now operator of the haunted attraction Asylum 49, was originally a skeptic of the Tooele hauntings. But after experiencing the paranormal activity there firsthand, he quickly became a believer and has even adopted the number three into the rituals that are part of Asylum 49.

The intensity of the Tooele Hospital hauntings eventually led to a full-scale exorcism, conducted during a paranormal investigation. The sheer amount of supernatural activity had become so overwhelming, investigators sought to cleanse the building of any malevolent forces. By the end of the ritual, it was reported that the exorcism had been successful, though many believe that while some spirits may have been banished, Tooele Hospital remains far from free of paranormal activity. To this day, guests who visit Asylum 49 report experiencing strange phenomena—floating orbs of light, unexplained mists forming in empty rooms, and the unnerving sensation of being watched. Some have even claimed to hear whispers in the dead of night or to have been touched by unseen hands.

THE SMURL FAMILY HAUNTING

WEST PITTSTON, PENNSYLVANIA
1973

In 1973, Jack and Janet Smurl, along with their two young daughters, Dawn and Heather, and Jack's parents, John and Mary, were forced from their home after it was severely damaged by a flood. They moved into a modest duplex in West Pittston, Pennsylvania, where Jack's parents lived in the right half of the house, while Jack, Janet, and their daughters occupied the left. The house was far from perfect—a true fixer-upper—but the family worked hard to paint, repair, and make it their own. They were eager to start fresh after their recent hardship.

During remodeling, about eighteen months after moving in, the family encountered several unsettling incidents. At first, they were subtle and easy to dismiss: Tools mysteriously disappeared and then reappeared, old stains on the walls bled through fresh paint, and strange, foul odors would suddenly fill the air before vanishing. One day, kitchen appliances inexplicably caught fire despite being unplugged, and Jack's television burst into flames. Since it was an old house, the family brushed off these incidents as random coincidences...until they no longer could. To their utter disbelief, the Smurls found deep, animallike scratches in the sink and bathtub of their newly remodeled bathroom. About a year later, the Smurls' daughter Dawn regularly saw people floating around her bedroom at night. Janet endured several horrifying encounters, including a malevolent force that molested her in her sleep. Jack didn't escape these disturbances. One night, as he lay in bed with Janet, he heard what sounded like a young woman whispering. When he turned to his wife, he was horrified to see a shadowy figure run up her body. On top of all this, black masses appeared throughout the house, leaving an oppressive atmosphere in their wake.

Nevertheless, life kept moving forward for the Smurls. By 1977, the family welcomed twin daughters, Shannon and Carin. But this growing family was also growing concerned. The toilets flushed on their own, footsteps echoed up and down the stairs when no one was there, drawers opened and closed by themselves, and rocking chairs swayed as if occupied by an unseen presence. They could no longer ignore the signs—something evil haunted their home.

The disturbances kept escalating. The house would suddenly become ice cold, a chill that seeped into their bones. Jack's parents, John and Mary, heard loud, abusive arguments coming from Jack and Janet's side of the house—only to find out there had been no quarrels. While in the basement one day, Janet heard her name being called, but when she searched the house, she realized she'd been alone the entire time.

Two days later, the house turned ice cold once again. This time, Janet encountered a terrifying black figure with a human shape but no facial features. The figure kept moving, passed through the kitchen wall, and then appeared to Mary on the opposite side of the house.

Eventually, the disturbances became violent. Out of nowhere, a ceiling fan came crashing down on Shannon, injuring her on the same night that her sister Heather was to be confirmed in the Catholic faith. Another night, after Jack and Janet had been intimate, Janet was violently pulled off the bed and began levitating in the air. Jack lay paralyzed, unable to help, as he gagged on a vile, putrid odor that filled the room.

The family's German shepherd, Simon, was repeatedly thrown across the room and slammed into walls by an unseen force. Throughout the day, terrifying voices echoed through the house, and wild scratching sounds came from within the walls. One night, while Shannon was asleep, she was violently tossed out of her bed and hurled down the stairs.

It wasn't just the Smurls being haunted; soon their neighbors began reporting bloodcurdling screams and bizarre noises coming from the house—when the family wasn't home.

Enough was enough. The Smurls were determined to fight back against whatever was tormenting them. In January 1986, Janet contacted Ed and Lorraine Warren, renowned paranormal investigators and demonologists. After hearing about the Smurls' experiences, the Warrens responded quickly, arriving with Rosemary Frueh, a registered nurse and psychic, and began their investigation.

Their process started with an in-depth interview. The Warrens asked the Smurls about their family's happiness, religious beliefs, and whether they had ever practiced satanism, used a Ouija board, or intentionally invited spirits into their home. After ruling out these possibilities, the Warrens and Frueh conducted a thorough walk-through of the house.

According to the Warrens, they detected the presence of four entities: three minor spirits and one powerful, malevolent demon. With no signs of family dysfunction or any intentional summoning of spirits, they theorized the demon had been dormant in the house for decades. Its activity was likely triggered by the emotional charge released by the girls entering puberty. With this conclusion, the Warrens began their efforts to rid the Smurls of the sinister forces that plagued their home.

The Warrens attempted to provoke the demon by playing religious music and reciting prayers, hoping to confront the malevolent force. The entity reacted violently, shaking mirrors and dressers and even spelling out vile messages such as, "You filthy bastard, get out of this house." Unfortunately, things only got worse.

Jack Smurl was assaulted by a grotesque succubus that appeared as an old woman with a young body, bloodred eyes, and green gums. Janet was sexually assaulted by an incubus. Ed Warren was also attacked—he was choked and later suffered severe flu-like symptoms. On top of everything, disturbing piglike noises continuously echoed from within the walls, a common sign of demonic infestation.

Desperate for help, the Warrens enlisted Bishop McKenna, who had previously assisted them with over fifty exorcisms. Despite all their efforts, the activity worsened. One of the twins, Carin, became gravely ill with a high fever, while Dawn narrowly escaped being sexually assaulted by the entity. Both Janet and Mary found unexplained slashes and bite marks on their arms, a chilling reminder of the demon's growing power. The demon relentlessly tormented the Smurls, even following them on trips to the Poconos and harassing Jack at work.

Ed Warren explained to the family that they had entered the second stage of demonic oppression—a critical point where if the activity couldn't be stopped, possession and even death could follow.

Despite the mounting danger, the local church continued to deny their requests for assistance. Feeling they had no other option, the Smurls appeared anonymously on the Philadelphia talk show *People Are Talking* to share their story. However, this public exposure only provoked the demon further, intensifying the family's nightmare.

The demon levitated Janet and violently slammed her against a wall. It appeared to Jack as a terrifying piglike creature walking on two legs. One night, a human hand emerged from the couple's mattress and gripped Janet tightly by the back of her neck. Jack suffered yet another assault by the entity. Despite the danger they were in, the Smurls were determined to share their story.

They gave an interview to the *Wilkes-Barre Sunday Independent*, bringing even more attention to their home and turning it into a media spectacle. Crowds gathered outside, and the Smurls were subjected to widespread skepticism. People spread rumors that accused the Smurls of fabricating their story for financial gain, saying they were only doing this for potential book or movie deals.

Needing further help, the Smurls reached out to a medium, Mary Alice Rinkman, and invited her to their home. She confirmed the Warrens' findings, identifying four spirits in the house. One was an elderly woman named Abigail, while another was a dark-haired man named Patrick, who had murdered his wife and her lover before being executed by a mob. The third spirit remained unnamed, and the fourth was a powerful, malevolent demon.

Meanwhile, the Warrens had organized a mass exorcism with multiple priests, and Bishop McKenna returned for a final attempt to cleanse the house. This time, it seemed to work. For three months, the Smurls experienced peace—no disturbances, no attacks. But just before Christmas in 1986, Jack encountered the black entity again. It was preparing him for the third and most dangerous stage: possession. Despite constant prayers, the family and their house continued to be plagued with loud banging, foul odors, and violent assaults.

Reaching their breaking point, the Smurls left their home and moved to another town. Sadly, the demon followed them to their new house, continuing to torment the family until 1989, when a church-sanctioned exorcism finally brought the activity to an end.

What the Smurl family endured was nothing short of a living nightmare—a relentless, otherworldly terror that invaded every corner of their lives. The Smurls' suffering serves as a chilling reminder of how little control we might have against the unseen.

NO
YES
ABCDEFGHIJKLM
NOPQRSTUVWXYZ
34567890
GOOD BYE

ESTEFANÍA AND THE OUIJA BOARD

MADRID, SPAIN
1990

When Estefanía Gutiérrez Lázaro was eighteen, her grandfather summoned his children and grandchildren to his deathbed for what would be his final farewell. However, his action was more out of obligation than love, as he had little fondness for his family. In his final moments, he whispered a chilling message to Estefanía: "If I cannot harm you in this life, I will do it in the next." Though the words were unsettling, Estefanía may not have fully grasped their gravity at the time.

Soon after Estefanía's grandfather's death, the boyfriend of one of Estefanía's friends was killed in a motorcycle accident. Overcome with grief, Estefanía and her friends tried to contact the deceased boyfriend using a Ouija board while at school. It wasn't long before their séance was interrupted by a teacher, and the Ouija board broke in all the commotion. When the board shattered, an unnatural, dark smoke reportedly rose from its broken pieces—and Estefanía inhaled it.

Not long after, Estefanía began suffering from severe convulsions that left her family terrified and desperate for answers. During these episodes, her body would stiffen unnaturally, her eyes would roll back until they turned completely white, and foam would spill from her mouth. She experienced chilling visions, too, telling her mother, Concepción, that she was being stalked by shadowy, silhouetted figures. These dark entities lurked around her, constantly watching.

One night, Estefanía violently lashed out at her family in a fit of rage and then immediately blacked out, claiming to have no memory of the attack. Alarmed, Concepción sought help from numerous hospitals and specialists, but none could find anything wrong with Estefanía. Although her symptoms seemed to resemble epilepsy, every test came back inconclusive. Eventually, medical professionals attributed her condition to a psychotic breakdown, but others were convinced it was something darker: possession. Some even speculated her late grandfather had a hand in her torment.

For months, Estefanía endured increasingly severe episodes, each one worse than the last. By 1991, her visions had intensified, too. She confessed to her family that the shadowy figures started speaking to her, urging her to join them. Just days later, nineteen-year-old Estefanía passed away under mysterious circumstances, leaving her family shattered and searching for answers.

Unfortunately for the Gutiérrez family, as they tried to grieve the loss of Estefanía, their sorrow was soon overshadowed by whatever had been tormenting their daughter. Its attention was now on the family.

Days after Estefanía's death, strange knocking noises echoed from her empty bedroom, accompanied by a haunting voice repeatedly calling out, "Mama, Mama." When Concepción finally entered the room, she found Estefanía's belongings scattered chaotically across the floor, as if hurled by an unseen force. The next night, the sound of an old man's laughter echoed through the house.

Disembodied voices, random temperature drops, and unexplainable occurrences became part of their daily lives. One day, Estefanía's father, Máximo, was playing with his young son, Maximilian, and without warning, an invisible force picked up Maximilian and threw him across the room. The Gutiérrez family was no longer alone.

One evening, as they sat in the living room, a door suddenly burst open, followed by a series of loud, aggressive knocks reverberating from every wall in the house. Panicked, Concepción and Máximo pushed a sofa against the door to keep it shut. But a powerful gust of wind forced the door open, sending the sofa—and the family—flying across the room. Amid the chaos, an object also flew into the room: a framed photo of Estefanía.

When Concepción picked up the photo, she screamed in horror as the picture of her daughter spontaneously burned in her hands, splitting Estefanía's face down the middle. Oddly, the frame remained untouched by the fire.

For months after Estefanía's death, doors kept violently slamming shut, appliances turned on and off at random, and shadowy figures began to manifest. At night, these otherworldly beings would crawl around the family's beds and furniture, filling the home with an oppressive, sinister presence.

One day, while Maximilian was making lunch, he heard a sharp whistling sound. He ducked instinctively, narrowly avoiding a sharpened piece of wood that pierced a sausage hanging on the wall. Estefanía's sisters described several encounters with a faceless shadowy figure that dragged itself across the floor, and flung the girls' dolls around the room, leaving them in utter terror. By this point, the family was living in constant fear. With no other options, they decided to seek help from experts, hoping to rid their home of the dark presence that had taken over their lives.

Psychics, investigators, and religious officials all visited the Gutiérrez home in a desperate attempt to rid it of the relentless paranormal activity. During one of these sessions, a medium claimed to be possessed by the malevolent spirit of Estefanía's grandfather.

According to the medium, while the grandfather's vengeful spirit was tormenting the family, Estefanía's spirit was also present, fighting to protect her loved ones. Not only was she trying to stop her grandfather, but she was also shielding her family from the other sinister entities that had taken hold of their home.

A month later, more than a year after Estefanía's untimely death, the family reached their breaking point. Máximo, utterly desperate, made a frantic call to the police, claiming his house was haunted and that his family was in immediate danger.

At first, his story was dismissed, but Máximo refused to give up. During his next call to the police, he passed the phone to every family member, who each provided horrifying accounts of what they'd endured. They described crucifixes spinning upside down, shadowy figures stalking the house, and an overwhelming sense of dread. Hearing the desperation in their voices, Officer José Negri decided to finally take this family seriously. He, along with three other officers, headed to the Gutiérrez home expecting to dismiss their claims but instead witnessed unexplained phenomena that left them shaken. After their search, the officers left abruptly, telling the family there was nothing they could do to help. The police report, written by Officer Negri, does, however, give credibility to the family's unsettling accounts.

> "We were found amidst a rare and mysterious situation, that being seated in the company of all the family, we could hear and observe a perfectly closed cabinet door, something which we verified afterwards, open suddenly in a completely unnatural way. This started a series of suspicious events that were witnessed by the chief inspector and the three other police officers present."

> "Whilst still in a state of shock, a powerful noise came from the terrace, where we could prove there was no one present. The suspicious events then increased in quantity and severity, taking the investigation up to an unexpected level."

"Moments later they could hear and see that, on the tablecloth on a small telephone table, there appeared a brown stain, which the chief inspector identified as drool."

"During the search of the rooms of the home, the phenomena which we have been referencing was observed. A wooden crucifix rotated and was ripped off the wall. One of the daughters picked up the crucifix from the floor and attached it behind the door to the room. Suddenly and strangely three scratch marks appeared next to the cross."

For the Gutiérrez family, this was yet another devastating blow. Desperate, they tried everything they could think of—consulting more experts, turning to religious officials, and even performing their own rituals—but nothing seemed to work. The haunting continued, unabated, leaving the family mentally and emotionally drained.

In time, the Gutiérrez family made the difficult decision to leave their home, abandoning the place where they had once lived happily before Estefanía's death. Fortunately, when they moved, the relentless paranormal activity did not follow them, allowing them to finally find peace. This case of possession in Vallecas remains one of Spain's most infamous and chilling accounts of paranormal phenomena, a haunting story that continues to captivate and terrify those who hear it.

THE KIDS WHO WALKED ON WALLS

GARY, INDIANA
2011

Latoya Ammons moved with her three children—aged seven, nine, and twelve—and her mother, Rosa Campbell, to a modest rental home with dreams of a fresh start and a brighter future. The family hoped this move would mark a positive turning point in their lives. Their small, unassuming house seemed perfect—affordable, quiet, and tucked away in a residential neighborhood.

They moved in, and almost immediately, strange events began to occur. Despite it being a harsh November Indiana winter—a time when insects were virtually nonexistent—swarms of flies kept appearing around the house. No matter how many flies they killed, they kept returning.

Next, Latoya and Rosa began hearing footsteps echoing through the house, often coming from the basement and moving up into the kitchen. They even heard the basement door opening and closing on its own. Each time they checked, the door was locked, and no one was there—but the sounds persisted.

One night, Rosa awoke to the shadowy figure of a man pacing back and forth in her bedroom, staring straight at her. Overcome with fear, she leaped out of bed and the figure vanished—but it left behind large, wet footprints on her bedroom floor. Despite such unsettling events, the family tried to push forward and make their new house a home.

Unfortunately, whatever was haunting them seemed determined to drive them out. Four months after moving in, the family was hosting friends to mourn the loss of a loved one. The gathering kept Latoya up into the late hours of the night, and around 2:00 a.m., when she went to check in on her daughter, guests heard her screaming hysterically. Her daughter, who was in her grandmother's room along with a friend, was levitating above the bed, completely unconscious.

When the guests heard Latoya's screams, they rushed to the room, several of them witnessing her daughter's levitating body. In a desperate attempt to help, they prayed. Slowly, Latoya's daughter descended back onto the bed. When she opened her eyes, she had no memory of what had happened.

Terrified and desperate for answers, the family decided they needed help. They reached out to countless churches, but their pleas were mostly ignored—except by one. A church representative agreed to visit the house and confirmed the presence of spirits, advising the family to cleanse the house with bleach and ammonia. Beyond the church, Latoya also consulted with mediums, who confirmed the house was filled with an evil presence and was inhabited by as many as two hundred spirits and demons.

Unfortunately, moving out was not an option—they simply couldn't afford it. So, the family followed the advice of the church and mediums, doing everything they could to cleanse it. However, just three days after the cleansing, the demons returned with even greater fury. The children started speaking in deep, guttural voices, whispering ominous phrases like, "It's time to die" and "I will kill you." When they spoke, their eyes would bulge unnaturally, and their mouths would twist into eerie, unsettling smiles.

Latoya's twelve-year-old daughter recounted being held down and choked by an unseen force, whispering that she would be dead in twenty minutes. Her seven-year-old son was found sitting alone in a dark closet, talking to someone invisible. When asked who he was speaking to, he replied, "We're talking about what it feels like to be killed."

Terrified for her children's safety, Latoya brought them to their family doctor, Dr. Geoffrey Onyeukwu. The doctor initially believed the family was experiencing delusions and hallucinations, but he changed his mind when the kids began exhibiting signs of demonic possession during their visit. Latoya's seven-year-old son began growling and cursing at Dr. Onyeukwu, rising from the floor and slamming his head into the wall, as if being thrown by an unseen force. He passed out and couldn't be revived until he was taken to the hospital.

When he regained consciousness, he turned violent, thrashing around uncontrollably. It took five adults to finally restrain him, and as they stood over him, he fixed his gaze on his older brother and said, "It's time to die. I will kill you." His nine-year-old brother's face twisted into a sinister grin. Then, defying all logic, he glided across the floor and up the wall, leaving everyone stunned and horrified.

The relentless torment began to take its toll on the children. They started missing numerous days of school, raising concerns with authorities, and prompting the police to intervene. Child Protective Services (CPS) visited the home, and during their visit, they witnessed Latoya's seven-year-old son walking up a wall, flipping over Rosa, and landing effortlessly. This terrified the CPS workers, so much so that they ran out of the house and ultimately deemed the children were in imminent danger. CPS placed them in emergency protective custody, separating them from Latoya. Following the separation, police officers were sent to check in on Latoya at her home, where they experienced radio malfunctions, witnessed a mysterious white, smoky figure, and even captured a ghostly voice saying, "Hey."

Word of the family's plight eventually reached a local priest, Father Michael Maginot. Feeling compelled to intervene and convinced that supernatural forces were at work, he offered to perform an exorcism. Initially, Father Maginot believed Latoya's seven-year-old son was possessed, as his behavior had grown increasingly erratic and violent. However, after speaking with Latoya and Rosa at their home, he concluded that Latoya herself was the primary target of possession and the demonic attacks. He claimed she was under the control of the powerful demon Beelzebub, also referred to as "The Lord of Flies."

Over the course of several weeks, Father Maginot performed three exorcisms on Latoya—two in English and one in Latin. After the final ritual, he declared Latoya free from the grip of the demons. After the exorcisms proved successful, Latoya dedicated herself to regaining custody of her children. She underwent evaluations and worked tirelessly to meet the requirements set by authorities. By November 2012, her children were back in her care. Determined to leave their traumas behind, the family moved to Indianapolis and focused on rebuilding their lives. For them, the "Demon House" and its horrifying memories were a thing of their past.

The infamous house in Gary, Indiana, was ultimately demolished in 2016, erasing the physical reminder of the events that had plagued the Ammons family.

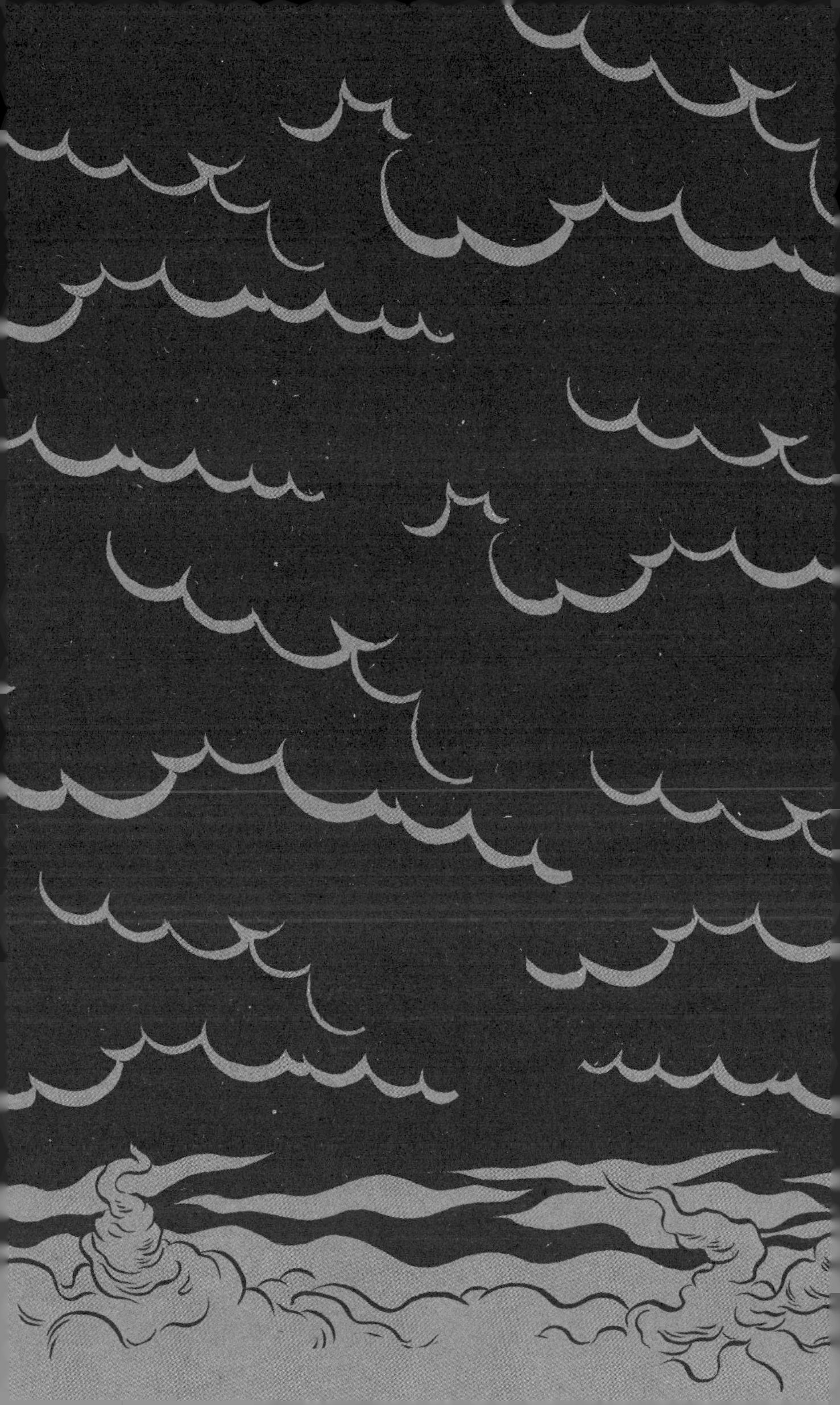

THE BUNK BEDS FROM HELL

HORICON, WISCONSIN

1987

In April 1986, the Tallman family—Allen, Debbie, and their three children, a son and two daughters—moved into their dream home in Horicon, Wisconsin. For a while, life seemed perfect, and the family of five was thrilled to be settling in.

The next February, while browsing a secondhand store for new furniture, the Tallmans found the perfect bunk bed for their children. Allen assembled the bunk beds in the basement, leaving them there until they were ready to move into one of the kids' rooms. Only a few days after bringing the bunk bed into their home, the children, who were rarely sick, fell very ill. Debbie found herself taking them to the doctor multiple times a week, baffled by their persistent ailments. By May, the bunk bed was finally moved into a room upstairs, next to where their son slept.

That night, their son's radio began switching channels on its own, the dial visibly moving back and forth. Frightened, the boy ran out of his room and straight down to the living room to tell his parents. His face pale with terror, Allen and Debbie reassured him that it was nothing more than his imagination. To ease his fears, they removed the radio from his room before sending him back to bed.

A few weeks later, Allen was painting the basement when Debbie called him upstairs to take a break for lunch. He carefully set his paintbrush on the edge of the pan and went upstairs. When he returned, however, his stomach dropped. The brush, which he had left resting on the pan, was now submerged handle-first into the paint can. Allen, knowing with absolute certainty that he hadn't placed it there, disregarded this, unwilling to believe anything unusual was happening.

Then one night, as their daughter lay sleeping in the bunk bed, she awoke to a menacing old woman with glowing red eyes. The figure moved creepily around the room, creating sudden bursts of flames that vanished quickly. Night after night, the old woman appeared, pacing through the darkness, her fiery eyes burning into the little girl's memory. Debbie, though unsettled by her daughter's claims, again dismissed them as nothing more than a young child's vivid imagination.

But once again, their son woke up in the middle of the night, this time screaming in utter terror. He too had seen the horrifying woman with the glowing red eyes. With tears streaming down his face, he described her in the same eerie detail as his sister.

Fearing for their family, Allen and Debbie turned to their pastor, Wayne Dobratz. As soon as he entered their home, an overwhelming sense of dread washed over him. He felt an oppressive force lurking in the air, a presence so dark that he believed it to be the work of the devil himself. Deeply disturbed, he urged the family to strengthen their faith and begin attending church regularly, warning them that spiritual warfare was the only way to fight against such malevolent forces.

Unfortunately, the fact that the family attended church only seemed to anger the presence more. Strange, guttural voices whispered through the house in the dead of night. The sounds were low, inhuman, and laced with malice. Doors slammed shut violently, rattling the walls, only to creak open moments later. The children, already tormented by the red-eyed woman's nightly visits, found themselves trapped in an unrelenting cycle of fear. The entity was growing stronger and more aggressive, and it was clear it had no intention of leaving.

It was the week before Christmas, what should have been a time filled with joy, as it was their first Christmas in the house. Instead, it was filled with dread. Their son woke up screaming, this time also sobbing uncontrollably and drenched in sweat. He had seen another terrifying vision, though he could barely get the words out through his panic. This was the final straw for Allen—he had reached his breaking point. He stormed into the living room, fists clenched, enraged.

Enough was enough. With every ounce of his being, he bellowed, "GET OUT OF MY HOUSE!" his words daring the entity to respond. For several weeks, the family went without any disturbances. Allen thought he had won. But the presence lingered, intentionally patient. It waited. As Allen returned home late from work one night, he heard something at the front door—a voice whispering "Hey" in the darkness.

Allen's heart pounded in his chest as his eyes darted around the yard in the empty night. No one was there. But as he turned to head inside, the voice returned—this time louder, more urgent. Allen spun around, his breath caught in his throat. And that's when he saw his garage engulfed in flames. The fire raged, casting flickering shadows across the snow-covered ground. Allen's face suddenly felt hot as he staggered backward in shock. But as he turned to run inside for help, the flames vanished.

There was no fire. No smoke. No damage. The garage was perfectly intact, as if nothing had ever happened. But something had happened. Allen knew, in that moment, that whatever was tormenting them was far beyond his understanding. He was powerless against it. He could, however, protect his family. Allen started sleeping on the floor in his daughters' room; they were terrified and were having trouble sleeping through the night. He hoped his presence would provide some sense of comfort and safety. But the entity had no intention of stopping. And now, it had its sights on Allen.

One night, Allen awoke to an eerie, unnatural mist slowly creeping across his daughters' room. A cold chill ran down his spine as the fog thickened, swirling around him like something alive. Then, from within the dense haze, a voice—deep, guttural, and filled with malice—cut through the silence. "YOU'RE DEAD." The words echoed in his mind, paralyzing him with sheer terror. The next thing he knew, he was in the kitchen with Debbie, his body trembling uncontrollably. He couldn't speak. He couldn't explain what had just happened. His face was soaked in tears, his breath coming in ragged gasps. The fear had consumed him entirely.

Days passed, but the weight of that horrifying experience never left him. He knew the entity wasn't done with him. One evening, knowing he'd be working late, Allen asked a relative to stay in the room with his daughters until he got home. The relative agreed, though he was skeptical. He had heard the family's chilling stories but didn't believe them. He assumed it was just paranoia, until he too saw the burning woman.

The moment his eyes locked onto the terrifying figure, a blood-curdling scream ripped from his throat. At that moment, all doubt was gone. Whatever plagued the Tallman family was real.

For Debbie, that was the final straw. She grabbed the children and fled into the frigid winter night, refusing to spend another second in the house. Weeks later, the Tallman family took the bunk beds to a private dump and had them destroyed. Convinced that their nightmare was tied to them, they refused to chance another family using them ever again.

We may never know what really happened inside that house during those nine months, but one thing is certain—a once-happy family was driven out by something no one can explain.

GHOSTS OF THE PAST

ST. FRANCISVILLE, LOUISIANA 1800S TO TODAY

In 1796, David Bradford, a general during the Revolutionary War, purchased land in St. Francisville, Louisiana, and built his home, the infamous Myrtles Plantation, originally naming it "Laurel Grove." While David lived alone on the plantation for several years, he eventually brought his family and enslaved laborers to help manage the property. Following David's death, the plantation passed to his widow, Elizabeth Bradford. In 1817, Elizabeth handed control of the plantation to Clarke Woodruff, who was married to her and David's daughter Sarah Matilda. During Clarke's time running the plantation, he expanded the number of enslaved people working on the plantation and took a particular interest in an enslaved teenage girl named Chloe. Chloe knew that denying Clarke's advances would lead to brutal punishment, so she had no choice but to comply. This coerced relationship lasted for several years, Chloe living in constant fear of Clarke's wife finding out and punishing her severely. To protect herself, Chloe began eavesdropping on conversations around the plantation, hoping to gain information that might protect her position.

One day, Clarke caught Chloe listening at a door. In a fit of rage, he ordered that Chloe's ear be cut off as punishment. From then on, Chloe was forced to wear a green turban to hide her severed ear. Humiliated and angry, Chloe began plotting revenge. One evening, while Clarke was away and his family was gathered for dinner, Chloe allegedly slipped poison into their food. Two days later, Clarke's wife, Sarah, and two of his children were found dead. The other enslaved people, knowing what Chloe did, were terrified of what would happen when Clarke returned. Fearing for their own lives, they took swift and brutal action. A group of enslaved men seized Chloe, dragged her to a large oak tree on the plantation, and hanged her. After ensuring she was dead, they cut down her body and threw it into the nearby river to erase any evidence of the crime. But Chloe's spirit wasn't erased.

It wasn't until the 1970s, when the Myrtles Plantation was purchased by the Meyers family, that its reputation as a haunted hot spot truly took hold. The Meyers family opened the plantation as a bed-and-breakfast, hoping to draw in visitors intrigued by the plantation's dark past. But almost immediately after opening to the public, guests started reporting faint whispers and strange knocking sounds coming from empty rooms and ghostly apparitions appearing late at night—most frequently of a young girl wearing a green turban, her face partially obscured. The figure was often seen standing in doorways, peering through windows, or walking the halls. Many came to believe this figure was the spirit of Chloe, whose tragic story had by then become a full-blown local legend.

In 1992, the owner of the Myrtles Plantation took a photograph of the property to secure an insurance policy for the house. The photo was forgotten for years until researchers asked to use it for a postcard. When they enlarged the image, they noticed the faint, shadowy outline of a young woman standing near one of the columns—a young woman wearing a turban.

But Chloe isn't the only spirit tied to the plantation. Several guests have reported seeing young girls dressed in period clothing standing in the upstairs windows, staring blankly at them before disappearing into thin air. Others have claimed to see the reflections of Clarke Woodruff's children appearing in mirrors next to the room where they died. Objects have been known to move on their own, and sudden cold spots have been felt in areas with no air conditioning or drafts.

Another well-known ghost at the Myrtles Plantation is William Winter, the only man confirmed to have been murdered on the property. William was reportedly shot on the porch of the house, stumbling inside and attempting to climb the staircase before collapsing on the seventeenth step and dying in the arms of his wife.

To this day, guests and staff claim to hear footsteps in the house's entrance, followed by the heavy thud of a body. Some have even claimed to see William's spirit making his desperate climb, only to vanish before their eyes.

The plantation's haunted reputation has been bolstered by numerous photographs of ghostly figures and mysterious shapes, countless reports of being watched, hearing disembodied voices, and even experiencing sudden nausea or chills while exploring the house and grounds. Paranormal investigators who have visited the plantation have captured strange voices on tape, unexplained cold spots, and objects moving on their own.

Shrouded in a dark history and chilling tales of the supernatural, it's clear why the Myrtles Plantation is often called the most haunted plantation in America.

THE JABOTICABAL HAUNTING

JABOTICABAL, BRAZIL
1965

In Jaboticabal, Brazil, Maria Jose Ferreira was an eleven-year-old child, growing up in what seemed to be a peaceful household, with a devout Catholic family. In December 1965, the family was gathered in their home when, out of nowhere, a brick appeared and violently flew across the room. Stunned and confused, Maria's family looked around for an explanation but couldn't find one. Then another brick. And another. Soon bricks were materializing out of thin air, crashing onto the floor and against the walls.

At first, they assumed it was a prank or cruel joke since the family had a similar stack of bricks in their backyard. But as the days passed and the bricks continued to appear inside their home—sometimes in locked rooms or spaces completely sealed off from the outside—the family realized this was no ordinary prank. Something unexplainable was happening within their walls.

Desperate for answers, they turned to the church, believing that an evil presence had infested their home. A priest was sent to assess the situation, and after listening to all their disturbing experiences, he decided to perform an exorcism. The family clung to the hope that this sacred ritual would bring them relief and cleanse their home of whatever force was tormenting them. Unfortunately, the exorcism failed and instead of bringing peace, it made the Ferreiras' situation escalate.

The attacks against Maria grew and became increasingly violent—she was struck by flying bricks, slapped, bitten, and even stabbed by dozens of sharp sewing needles. It was soon clear that Maria was at the center of the poltergeist's wrath, and the family was struggling to find ways to protect her.

Witnessing their distress and determined to help, a family friend reached out to a well-known spiritist named João Volpe, who was experienced in dealing with the supernatural. After studying Maria and the strange events surrounding her, João came to a startling conclusion—Maria was a natural medium, unknowingly acting as a conduit between the physical world and the spirit realm. He believed that her ability to communicate with spirits had inadvertently fueled the poltergeist's activity. According to João, Maria had spent years interacting with invisible friends, many of whom she had described as kind and playful. Unfortunately, this time something sinister had latched on to her.

Wanting to help, João offered to take Maria into his home, hoping he could find a way to put an end to the disturbances. For the first few days, everything was quiet—giving João hope that the nightmare had finally ended—but then the chaos returned. Whenever Maria was present, stones began flying through João's house, hurling themselves across the room with terrifying force. João kept count and was astonished to find that a total of 312 stones had materialized. At one point, a single stone inexplicably struck three members of his family on the head before dropping to the floor.

Maria soon realized that her invisible companions were capable of more than just destruction—they could bring her objects at will. If she asked for candy or small trinkets, they would simply appear at her feet. One day, as Maria and João were walking down the street, Maria casually mentioned that she wanted a brooch. Moments later, a brooch materialized at her feet, leaving João both astounded and deeply unsettled. At first, Maria found the strange phenomenon amusing, as if she had been given a special ability. But her fascination quickly turned to terror when it seemed that the more "gifts" she received, the more violent the poltergeist's attacks became. It was no longer just stones—glassware, crockery, and other household items were flung across rooms, shattering on impact. This relentless destruction lasted for three weeks, with no signs of stopping.

The unseen force also turned its attention to Maria again. It resumed its physical assaults, striking her with slaps and vicious bites that left deep marks on her skin. It began using large, heavy items as weapons against her—chairs were launched in her direction, a massive sofa was toppled as if to crush her, and a gas cylinder was hurled at her with alarming force. The violent attacks continued even as Maria tried to sleep. Drinking glasses and cups appeared over her mouth, as if something—or someone—was trying to suffocate her in the dead of night.

Then, exactly forty days after the first brick had been thrown, the sewing needles returned. But this time, they weren't just pricking her skin—they were being driven deep into her flesh with agonizing precision. At one point, doctors were forced to extract fifty-five needles from her body in a single procedure.

One day at school, Maria was sitting down for lunch when, without warning, the fabric of her clothes began to smolder and burn. Panic erupted as students and teachers rushed to put out the mysterious flames. That same day, João's bedroom inexplicably burst into flames, and as he tried to put it out, he suffered severe burns when he grabbed a pillow—only to discover that it was burning from the inside out. Maria was no longer alone in her torment, and the presence seemed intent on harming anyone who tried to help her.

While these assaults were terrifying on their own, there were whispers of even darker happenings. Though unconfirmed, it's been said that Maria may have also been subjected to attempted sexual assault by the unseen entity, adding yet another horrifying layer to her torment.

João worked with Maria in his home for a year, doing everything in his power to free her from the relentless supernatural torment. Although he was unable to banish the entity completely, he managed to lessen its intensity and provided Maria with some much-needed relief. Desperate for a permanent solution, João sought the help of Brazil's most renowned medium, Chico Xavier, hoping he could provide answers.

When Maria was brought before Chico, the spirits revealed to him that she was a witch, responsible for the suffering and deaths of many in the past. These spirits—her supposed victims—were exacting their revenge. While some interpreted this to mean Maria had been a powerful witch in a previous life, others saw it as a cruel, otherworldly punishment—one that would not end until the spirits had taken their full revenge.

After Maria's meeting with Chico, the worst of the poltergeist activity finally subsided, although objects would still occasionally be tossed through the air. These events were a grim reminder that whatever had plagued Maria wasn't completely gone. Despite this, life slowly began to return to some semblance of normalcy. By 1970, Maria moved back in with her mother, hoping for a fresh start and an escape from the horrors she had endured.

Sadly, only three days after returning home, Maria was found lifeless in her room, the victim of an apparent suicide. She had consumed a drink laced with pesticides and died instantly. Was this Maria's own doing, or had the spirits finally claimed her as their own?

In the wake of Maria's death, the haunting came to an end. Both the Ferreira family and João Volpe never reported another instance of paranormal activity again. It seemed that with Maria gone, its purpose had been fulfilled. To this day, many believe that what happened to Maria was the result of true, malevolent forces—forces that not only tormented her but ultimately took her life.

THE HAUNTING OF THE SKIRVIN HOTEL

OKLAHOMA CITY, OKLAHOMA

1910

Located in the heart of Oklahoma City, the Skirvin Hotel is reputedly one of the most haunted hotels in the world. Synonymous with ghost sightings and paranormal activity, the Skirvin has left both its guests and staff shaken to their core. Its original owner, William Skirvin, was a wealthy and influential oilman from Texas who wanted to expand his legacy by adding a luxury hotel to the growing capital city of Oklahoma. At the time, Oklahoma City only had one other hotel of that caliber; therefore, Skirvin saw an opportunity to create something truly opulent. His vision paid off, with the hotel opening its doors in 1910 and quickly becoming *the* place to stay for business tycoons, politicians, and celebrities. But with its rise in popularity came a dark undercurrent—one steeped in mystery and tragedy.

Over the decades, countless guests of the Skirvin have reported strange and haunting occurrences. At first, the activity seemed minor: footsteps echoing down empty hallways, disembodied voices in the dead of night, and sudden cold spots that would chill guests to the bone. Doors would slam shut on their own, and objects would move without explanation. Many guests brushed off these experiences, but for those who witnessed them firsthand, these occurrences felt terrifyingly real. Over the years, the activity was consistent and pervasive, spreading across different floors and rooms. However, there is one spirit at the heart of the Skirvin Hotel's haunting whose presence is felt most strongly.

According to legend, the haunting traces back to a dark secret involving William Skirvin himself: He had an affair with one of the hotel's maids—a young woman named Effie—and she became pregnant. Skirvin, fearing the fallout from a scandal that could ruin his reputation and financial standing, took drastic measures to silence her. He allegedly locked Effie in a room on the tenth floor, isolating her from the outside world to keep the pregnancy a secret. Effie gave birth to the child, giving her hope that she'd finally be released, but her hopes were crushed. She remained trapped, forced to care for her newborn in complete isolation. The emotional toll was overwhelming, and after weeks of confinement, Effie became hopeless and desperate. In a final, tragic act, Effie clutched her baby and jumped from the tenth-floor window, plummeting to her death.

Having much power and influence, it's said that Skirvin covered up the death of Effie and her baby, keeping it out of the papers and making sure no formal investigation was launched. But for those who knew the inner workings of the hotel, it was whispered about for years. Though the tragic story of Effie has never been officially confirmed, many believe her spirit still lingers in the Skirvin Hotel, and the countless reports of paranormal activity seem to support the story's truth. Guests and staff have described seeing a woman, dressed in a maid's uniform, wandering the halls of the tenth floor, often accompanied by the sound of a baby crying. Effie's presence is not subtle. She's known to interact directly with guests, sometimes even speaking to them in a clear, intelligent manner. Some guests have felt the sensation of being touched or have heard Effie's voice whispering directly into their ear. A few have even claimed to have woken up in the middle of the night to find Effie sitting at the foot of their bed, watching them with sorrowful eyes.

Despite the fear Effie's presence evokes, paranormal investigators believe her spirit is not malicious. Instead, they suspect Effie's spirit is seeking connection and understanding. Several psychics and mediums who have visited the hotel agree, feeling that Effie is not vengeful but rather lonely, seeking some form of resolution and peace. Many have theorized that she remains trapped in the hotel because her tragic story was never properly acknowledged, her death swept under the rug to protect Skirvin's legacy.

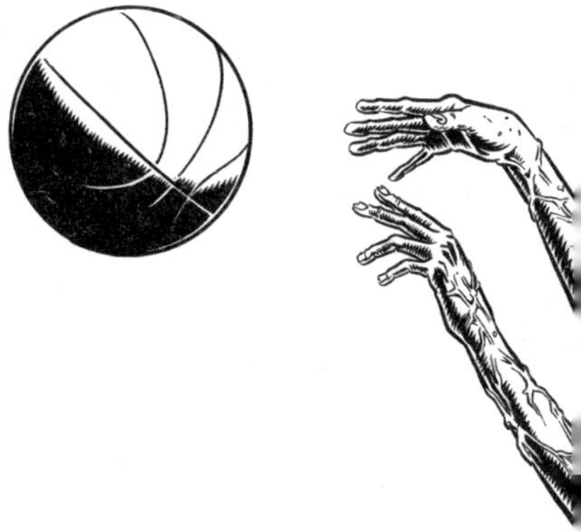

The Skirvin Hotel's paranormal reputation isn't just fueled by local lore and ghost stories. It's been validated several times by high-profile guests, particularly professional athletes. Over the years, the Skirvin has hosted numerous NBA teams, and many players have left the hotel with disturbing stories of ghostly encounters. In 2010, one of the most well-known incidents occurred when the New York Knicks were staying at the hotel before their game against the Oklahoma City Thunder. The Knicks suffered a devastating loss the following day. While at first the players said exhaustion was to blame for their poor performance, the players eventually opened up about what had really happened that night. Several team members described hearing strange creaking and groaning sounds coming from the walls and ceiling of their rooms. Some heard doors opening and closing on their own, while others described the overall energy of the hotel as unsettling and oppressive. The vibe was so disturbing that one Knicks player admitted to sleeping in another teammate's room out of fear.

The Knicks weren't the only team to experience strange happenings at the Skirvin. In 2013, the Baylor Bears women's basketball team stayed at the hotel while participating in the semifinals of their tournament. The team lost the game, and while none of the players directly blamed the Skirvin's haunting for the outcome, the connection was hard to ignore. Rumors quickly spread that the hotel's paranormal energy had psychologically affected the players, throwing them off their game.

In 2016, it was Los Angeles Lakers player Metta Sandiford-Artest (formerly known as Metta World Peace and Ron Artest) who had a strange, haunting experience at the Skirvin. The night before a game, Metta was in this room watching a movie when he felt something touching him—not once, but repeatedly. At first, he brushed it off, but the sensations continued and became impossible to ignore. Rather than panicking, Metta came to the conclusion that the Skirvin ghosts were messing with him. Taking the situation in stride, he even joked about it afterward, saying, "They touched me all over the place. I'm taking one of the ghosts to court for touching me in the wrong places." While his comment was meant to be humorous, it highlighted just how common Skirvin's ghostly experiences had become.

The fact that so many professional athletes—known for their physical toughness and mental fortitude—have been unnerved by their experiences at the Skirvin speaks volumes. For many teams, the Skirvin has become a sort of mental battlefield before they even step onto the court. The idea that the hotel is haunted has become so ingrained in sports culture that some teams have started requesting to stay elsewhere when playing in Oklahoma City, believing the Skirvin's energy could affect their performance.

The Skirvin Hotel's ghostly reputation seems to affect everyone, not just athletes. From business travelers to tourists, countless guests have reported similar experiences: strange sounds, eerie sensations, and the feeling of being watched. But for some reason, professional athletes seem to be particularly vulnerable to whatever forces linger within its walls. The Skirvin's legacy continues, with new reports surfacing regularly, making it clear that whatever haunts the Skirvin Hotel is not going anywhere anytime soon.

THE WRATH OF BATHSHEBA

HARRISVILLE, RHODE ISLAND

1971

In 1971, Roger and Carolyn Perron and their five daughters, Andrea, Nancy, Christine, Cindy, and April, moved into a fourteen-room farmhouse in Rhode Island. Built in 1736, the farmhouse had been vacant for several years and was in need of renovations, but the Perrons were excited for the opportunity it represented. Before moving in, the previous owners passed along an unnerving warning: "For the sake of your family, leave the lights on at night." The Perrons assumed this had to do with making sure no one fell down the home's steep staircase in the dark and didn't let the warning hinder their excitement.

At first, the strange occurrences were minor and did not raise immediate concern. Carolyn noticed small, almost playful disturbances: a broom disappearing, objects mysteriously shifting from their original locations, or the sound of scraping against kitchen kettles. Sometimes, after meticulously cleaning the kitchen, she would return to find small piles of dirt deliberately placed in the center of the floor.

Meanwhile, the Perron daughters began noticing ghostly figures throughout the house. Initially, these spirits seemed harmless, even welcoming. The girls grew fascinated by their presence, developing an unusual fondness for some of them. Mrs. Arnold, a woman who lived in the house during the 1800s, was said to be a gentle spirit, tucking the girls into bed at night and even leaving soft kisses on their foreheads. Another spirit, Johnny Arnold, was rumored to have taken his own life in the attic in the 1700s. The girls nicknamed him "Manny," and he would often move their toys and silently watch them play outside.

But as time passed, the family came to realize that not all the spirits were friendly. In time, spirits reeking of rotting flesh would invade the Perron family's bedrooms at precisely 5:15 every morning, disturbing their sleep in violent ways. These entities would lift beds off the ground and hurl the Perrons onto the floor, or sometimes specifically target the girls, yanking their hair and pulling at their limbs with an unnatural force. One night, a deep, guttural voice echoed through the home, warning the family that seven dead soldiers were buried within its walls. Telephone handsets would rise into the air and slam down violently. Furniture and household objects slid across rooms. Pictures twisted on the walls before being flung across the house. The family even witnessed an eerie, orange-colored liquid that looked like blood oozing from the walls.

Shaken, Carolyn decided to investigate the home's history. She discovered that, for eight generations, the house had remained in the same family, and many of its members had died tragic, untimely deaths. Several children drowned in the nearby creek, one was brutally murdered, and multiple people had hanged themselves in the attic—just like the spirit the girls called "Manny." But among all the restless souls that lurked in the farmhouse, one entity stood out as the most malevolent of them all: Bathsheba.

The Perrons described Bathsheba's appearance as utterly inhuman. Her face resembled a shriveled beehive, covered in cobwebs and devoid of any recognizable human features. Her head was sickly gray, misshapen, and leaned to one side as if her neck had been snapped. During the 1800s, Bathsheba lived in the house with her husband, Judson Sherman, and they had three children. Sadly, all three died in childhood. However, it wasn't her three children's deaths that made her infamous—it was the rumor that she sacrificed her infant. The child was found dead under her care, with a small but precise incision on the back of its head. Whispers spread through town, and soon the locals were convinced that Bathsheba was a witch. They claimed she practiced dark rituals, brutally tortured her servants, and had ultimately sold her soul to the devil.

Bathsheba's reputation was likely built on fear and envy. Many believed the accusations against her were driven by jealousy. She was a strikingly beautiful woman whose devoted husband provided for her. As the rumors spread through town, she was no longer seen as a wife or mother, but as a sadistic, evil woman who had committed unspeakable acts. The whispers turned to conviction, and in the end, Bathsheba took her own life, hanging herself from a tree behind the barn. Following her death, the rumors continued as some people claimed that her body turned to stone—a punishment from Satan himself, the price she had to pay for her beauty. They said that, in death, Bathsheba refused to relinquish her hold on the home. They said she considered herself the true mistress of the house, and when the Perrons moved in, she fixated her rage on Carolyn, whom she saw as a threat to her position.

Carolyn endured pinching, slapping, having objects hurled at her, and the sound of banging against her bed as she was commanded to leave. As the days turned to weeks, the attacks grew more vicious. One evening, as Carolyn lay on the couch, she suddenly felt a sharp, stabbing pain in her leg. When she looked down, she was horrified to see a sewing needle impaled deep into her calf. The message was clear: Bathsheba wanted her gone.

When Carolyn refused to leave, Bathsheba took her torment to the next level—she invaded her from within. The family watched in horror as Carolyn's behavior changed. Her complexion grew pale, her body frail, and her presence unsettling. Convinced that Carolyn was possessed, the Perrons knew they needed help. With nowhere else to turn, they reached out to the only people they believed could save them, paranormal investigators Ed and Lorraine Warren.

When Ed and Lorraine arrived at the Perron home, they immediately confirmed that Bathsheba's presence was not just haunting the house, it had taken hold of Carolyn. They quickly decided to conduct a séance to expel the dark force. The event that would be forever burned into the memory of her daughter Andrea. "That night, I thought I saw my mother die. It was the most terrifying night of all," said Andrea.

"She spoke in a voice we had never heard before, and a power not of this world threw her twenty feet into another room."

The séance did not bring relief—it only made things worse. Instead of driving Bathsheba away, it seemed to fuel her wrath. The energy in the house became darker and more aggressive. Roger, fearing for the safety of his family, demanded that the Warrens leave immediately.

After the séance, the Perrons continued to research the house and discovered they were not the first family to experience this horror. Every single family who lived in the farmhouse before them endured similar paranormal torment. One previous owner had even hired a contractor to renovate the house, but the renovations ended abruptly when the contractor heard bloodcurdling screams echoing within the empty house. Terrified, he fled the property, abandoning all his tools, and never returned. The owners were so disturbed by what had happened that they never moved in, leaving the house vacant for seven years until the Perrons arrived. Despite the relentless torment they faced, the Perrons were trapped. Financially, they had no choice but to stay. For eight long years, they endured the hauntings, never knowing when or if it would end.

Then, in 1979, just as suddenly as it had begun, the activity came to an inexplicable halt. The house fell silent. In 1980, with their finances finally stable, Carolyn demanded to leave, unwilling to risk the hauntings returning. Without hesitation, the family packed their belongings and moved to Georgia, leaving behind the house and the horrors that had nearly destroyed them.

In time, Andrea Perron felt compelled to share her story with the world, documenting her family's chilling experiences in a book titled *House of Darkness, House of Light*. During writing, Andrea discovered that the hauntings didn't end with her family. The next owner, Norma Sutcliffe, who purchased the farmhouse in 1983, also reported strange occurrences. Norma and her husband, Gerry, experienced unexplainable paranormal activity within the house: Doors would open and slam shut on their own, disembodied voices echoed through empty rooms, and on more than one occasion, they witnessed the eerie figure of an elderly woman slowly wandering through the house.

To this day, the Perron family remains uncertain about why they were tormented so viciously or why the hauntings suddenly ceased. The mystery behind the house and its lingering spirits remains unsolved. But one thing the Perrons are sure of: What they endured was nothing short of living hell.

THE BLACK HOPE CURSE

CROSBY, TEXAS
1982

In an upscale area of Texas, Sam and Judith Haney settled into what they felt was their dream home. It was also their dream neighborhood, filled with beautiful houses, community, and families like them, eager to start their new lives.

About a year after settling in, the Haneys decided to enhance their backyard with a swimming pool. One day, as construction was underway, an elderly man unexpectedly knocked on their front door, saying he had noticed their plans for the pool and felt compelled to warn them. Curious, Sam and Judith invited him into their backyard, allowing him to lead them to a specific area of the ground. Once they reached the spot, the man revealed that they were standing on a gravesite, which he knew because he had personally buried the bodies years ago when the land was still a cemetery.

The Haneys were shaken, so they decided to investigate. Sam, determined to uncover whatever lay beneath their yard, brought in a backhoe and began digging. As the hole deepened, he switched to digging by hand, and then—suddenly—he struck something solid. It was a set of pine boards.

His heart pounding, Sam carefully lifted the boards, revealing two wooden coffins. When he pried them open, he was met with a horrifying sight—decomposing human skeletons—confirming the old man's story. Without hesitation, Sam called the sheriff and the county coroner. When authorities arrived, they carried out an official exhumation, unraveling a dark history hidden beneath their home.

Most of the skeletal remains had deteriorated into fine powder, but twenty-five bone fragments were recovered. Inside one of the coffins were two wedding rings, still resting on the index finger of the skeleton. It was then that Sam and Judith realized the horrifying truth: They had desecrated a couple's grave.

Determined to right a wrong, the Haneys set out to uncover the identities of the deceased. Their research led them to Jasper Norton, a longtime resident who spent his youth digging graves in the area. Jasper revealed that the land their home—and many others—was built on had once been an African American cemetery known as Black Hope. Most of those buried there were formerly enslaved people, and the last recorded burial took place in 1939.

Using this information, the Haneys continued to investigate and eventually identified the couple as Betty and Charlie Thomas—both born into slavery and freed during the Civil War—who died in the 1930s and whose graves had long been forgotten. Overcome with remorse and seeking forgiveness, Sam and Judith took it upon themselves to rebury Betty and Charlie in their yard, hoping that a proper burial would bring their spirits peace.

Soon after the reburial, Judith noticed a strange glow coming from the clock in their bedroom. As she stepped closer, she realized it was sparking, but when she reached down to check it, she discovered it was unplugged.

On another occasion, while Sam was working a night shift, Judith was showering when she suddenly heard the sliding glass doors open and close, followed by a voice calling out, "What are you doing?" Assuming Sam had come home early, she quickly stepped out to check, only to find the house completely empty and the doors still locked. A chill ran down her spine.

Soon after, the couple noticed their belongings were mysteriously disappearing. One day, Judith reached for her favorite red shoes, but they were gone. She searched everywhere, growing increasingly frustrated. Sam joined in, tearing through the house, but the shoes had vanished. That is, until he stepped outside and spotted them, perfectly placed on the graves of Betty and Charlie Thomas. Then it occurred to him: It was Betty's birthday. The Haneys couldn't shake the feeling that this was Charlie's way of giving his wife a birthday gift from beyond the grave.

As the paranormal activity escalated, it became clear the Haneys weren't the only ones being haunted. Their neighbors shared disturbances of their own: Lights, faucets, and televisions flickered on their own. Disembodied whispers and chilling sounds filled the air. Several residents claimed to have seen ghostly apparitions roaming the neighborhood, as if the long-forgotten souls of Black Hope Cemetery were making their presence known once more.

Ben and Jean Williams, who moved into the neighborhood around the same time as Sam and Judith Haney, noticed that their plants were inexplicably dying. As they examined their yard, they discovered sinkholes forming near their flowerbeds, eerily shaped like coffins. Strange markings appeared on the trees nearby: arrows carved into the bark, all pointing toward the ground. A longtime resident eventually revealed that he had marked the tree years ago because his two sisters were buried beneath it. When Ben and Jean realized they had unknowingly disturbed the sisters' graves, they were overcome with guilt.

Shortly after, the couple began experiencing disturbing activity throughout their home. Sinister shadows slid across the walls, whispering voices echoed through empty rooms, and a foul, unrecognizable stench filled the air. Toilets flushed on their own, and at times, faint conversations could be heard, even when no one else was home. Jean felt a deep unease, convinced that the hauntings were tied to the graveyard beneath their home. "I absolutely believe that all of these things happened to us because we were on the graveyard," she later said. "And that we were simply going to be tormented until we left there." She wanted to leave. But Ben insisted they stay and fight.

Then, one night, Ben returned home from work and saw two ghostly figures moving down the hallway, heading straight for the bedroom. His heart pounded as he rushed in and found the apparitions standing over Jean as she lay in bed. Without hesitation, he lunged forward, leaping onto the bed—only for the spirits to vanish before his eyes. After six months of these hauntings, tragedy struck the Williams family. Several family members were diagnosed with cancer, and three of them lost their lives. Ben and Jean were convinced that the spirits in their home were to blame, certain they had been cursed for living on the desecrated land.

In the end, both families took legal action, hoping to seek justice for the dead and to hold the developers accountable for failing to disclose that their homes were built over a cemetery. The Haneys ultimately lost and were ordered to pay $50,000, forcing them into bankruptcy. The Williams, also unsuccessful in court, eventually took matters into their own hands. Jean grabbed a shovel and began digging up the graves in her backyard, determined to expose the truth. After just thirty minutes of digging, she suddenly fell ill. Her daughter, Tina, attempted to take over, but then, without warning, she suffered a massive heart attack. Despite doctors' efforts, Tina tragically passed away two days later. She was only thirty years old.

For Jean, there was no question—her daughter's death was the result of the vengeful spirits. Devastated, Ben and Jean ultimately left the neighborhood. Strangely, the current residents of the homes have reported no paranormal activity. To this day, no one can fully explain what tormented the Haneys and the Williams family—or why, after so much tragedy, the disturbances came to such an abrupt end.

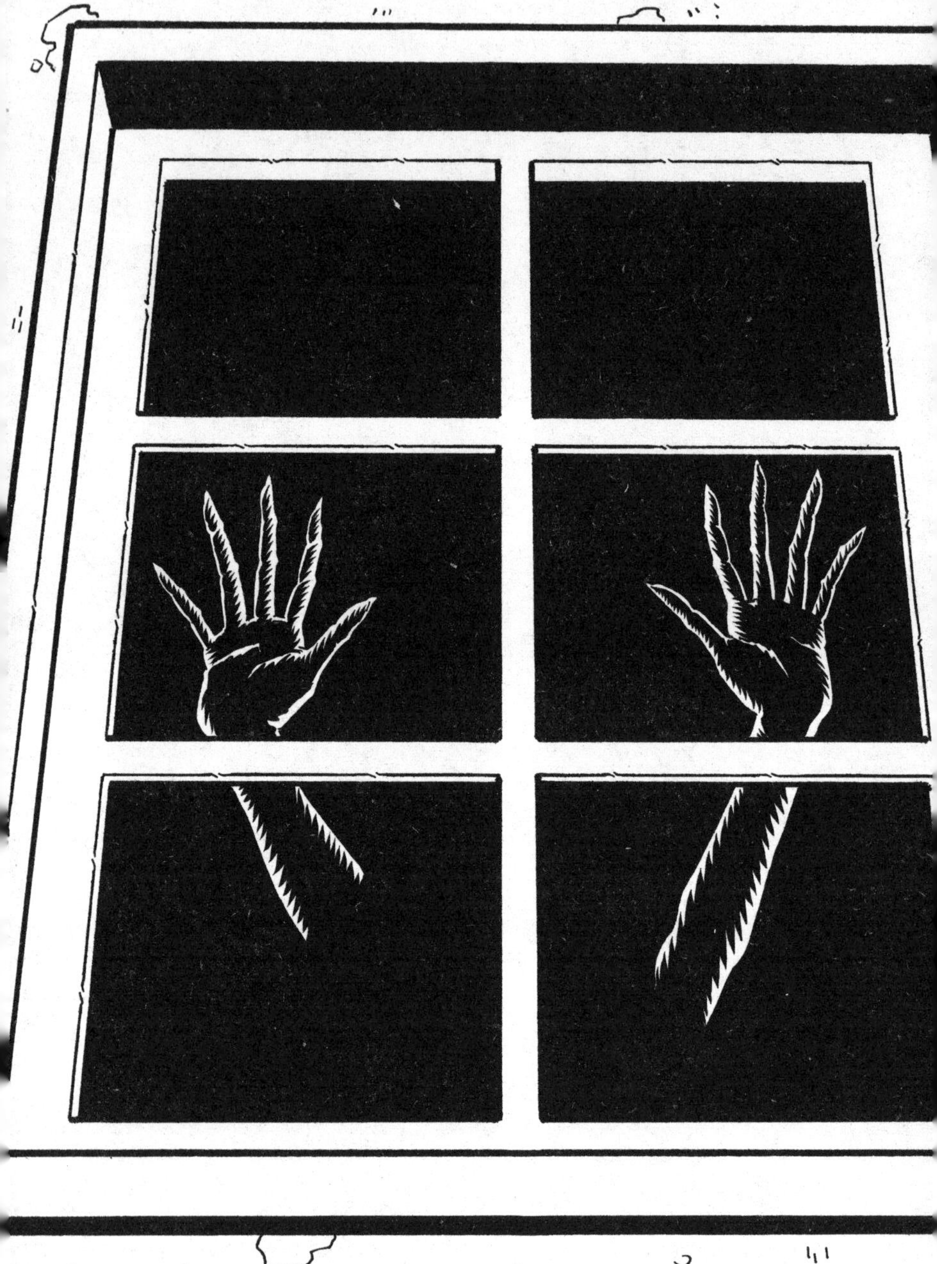

THE FUNERAL HOME HAUNTING

SOUTHINGTON, CONNECTICUT

1986

The Snedeker family, consisting of Carmen Reed, her husband, Allen Snedeker, their four children—Philip, Bradley, Allen Jr., and Jennifer—and Carmen's niece, Tammy, were searching for a home that would make their lives easier during a difficult time. Philip, their oldest son, had been diagnosed with Hodgkin's lymphoma, so the family had to frequently travel long distances from upstate New York to the University of Connecticut hospital for his treatments. The back-and-forth was both exhausting and financially draining, so they decided to move closer to the hospital, hoping to find some relief.

The Snedekers finally found the perfect home in Southington, Connecticut. It was spacious, affordable, and most importantly, just minutes from Philip's hospital. The process of moving and settling in went smoothly, and the family felt hopeful. But while exploring the basement, Carmen discovered a collection of funerary items, embalming equipment, and other tools used in mortuary practices. Throughout the rest of the house, they found drawers filled with creepy photos of corpses. Outside, they found a small graveyard. Shocked and disturbed, Carmen immediately called the landlord, Darrell Kern, demanding an explanation. That's when he finally revealed that the house was once the Hallahan Funeral Home—a former mortuary that had operated for decades. Despite the home's unsettling past, Philip and Bradley decided to make the basement their bedroom.

Philip was the first to experience the strange occurrences, claiming to see a young man with long black hair flowing down to his hips. At first, this figure would simply talk to him, but its words quickly became threatening. As time passed, the rest of the family began to experience their own terrifying encounters. Disembodied voices echoed through the house, and cold spots would appear in rooms without explanation. Shadowy silhouettes resembling the dead would manifest before their eyes.

One day, Carmen was mopping the floor when the water in her bucket suddenly turned into a deep red, bloodlike liquid that reeked of rotting flesh. Carmen also described seeing a spectral man with a gaunt face, high cheekbones, long black hair, and piercing black eyes. There was something incredibly powerful about his presence, and she felt an overwhelming sense of fear whenever he appeared.

Furthermore, Carmen and Allen both claimed they were physically violated by unseen forces—attacked, raped, and sodomized by an unknown entity. While the spirits violently tormented the adults, they seemed to develop a strange fixation on Philip, and his behavior began to change drastically. He became darker, more aggressive, and unpredictably violent. His once-loving nature turned cruel and menacing. He started lashing out at his younger siblings, inflicting disturbing punishments on them.

One day, Philip strapped his younger brother, Bradley, onto a gurney and spun him around wildly, ignoring his desperate pleas to stop. Another time, he locked Bradley inside a chest and walked away, leaving him trapped inside. It was clear that something was deeply wrong, and the Snedeker family feared they were losing their son.

When Philip attacked his cousin Tammy, he was hospitalized for forty-five days and ultimately diagnosed with schizophrenia. While under medical care, Philip spoke openly about the entities he had been seeing, detailing his experiences. To help him, the Snedekers sent Philip to live with relatives. Strangely, once he left the house, the visions and voices vanished completely. However, for the rest of the family, the nightmare was far from over.

Neighbors and visitors reported feeling an overwhelming sense of unease when approaching the property, with many claiming they had seen ghostly figures staring at them from the windows. The Snedekers knew they needed help. Out of desperation, they reached out to renowned paranormal investigators John Zaffis, Ed Warren, and Lorraine Warren.

The investigators started out by interviewing the family, but as they dug deeper into the home's history, they developed a disturbing theory. They believed that the former funeral workers engaged in necrophilia, which may have awakened a dark and malevolent presence. Not only that, they also suspected that several of the spirits belonged to the deceased individuals who had been embalmed in the family's basement when their house had operated as a funeral home.

To confirm their suspicions, the Warrens conducted several sessions to communicate with the entities. Throughout their time in the house, they experienced unexplainable drops in temperature, smelled the overwhelming stench of decay, and even witnessed shadowy apparitions lurking in the home. It became undeniably clear—this was not a simple haunting but a full-blown infestation of malevolent spirits intent on tormenting the family.

Realizing the severity of the situation, the Warrens sought the assistance of a priest to perform an exorcism on the home. On September 9th, 1988, the exorcism was carried out, and after an intense ritual, the dark presence was finally driven out. From that moment forward, the paranormal activity ceased entirely. Later that same year, the Snedeker family moved out of the house and never looked back.

Over time, skepticism began to overshadow the Snedekers' claims of being tormented by violent spirits. Despite this, the Snedeker family remained steadfast in their claims, insisting that the haunting was real and that they had suffered unimaginable torment in the house. They maintained that they had no control over how others chose to interpret their story, nor did they seek to change the minds of skeptics.

To them, the fear and trauma they endured left emotional and psychological scars that would never fully heal.

Regardless of where the truth lies, one undeniable fact remains—whatever the Snedekers experienced in that house profoundly affected them, shaping the rest of their lives. Their story has been retold in books, documentaries, and even a Hollywood adaptation, cementing its place in paranormal history. To this day, the Snedeker haunting remains one of the most infamous and controversial cases of alleged supernatural activity in American history, sparking discussions about the thin line between reality and fiction in the world of the unexplained.

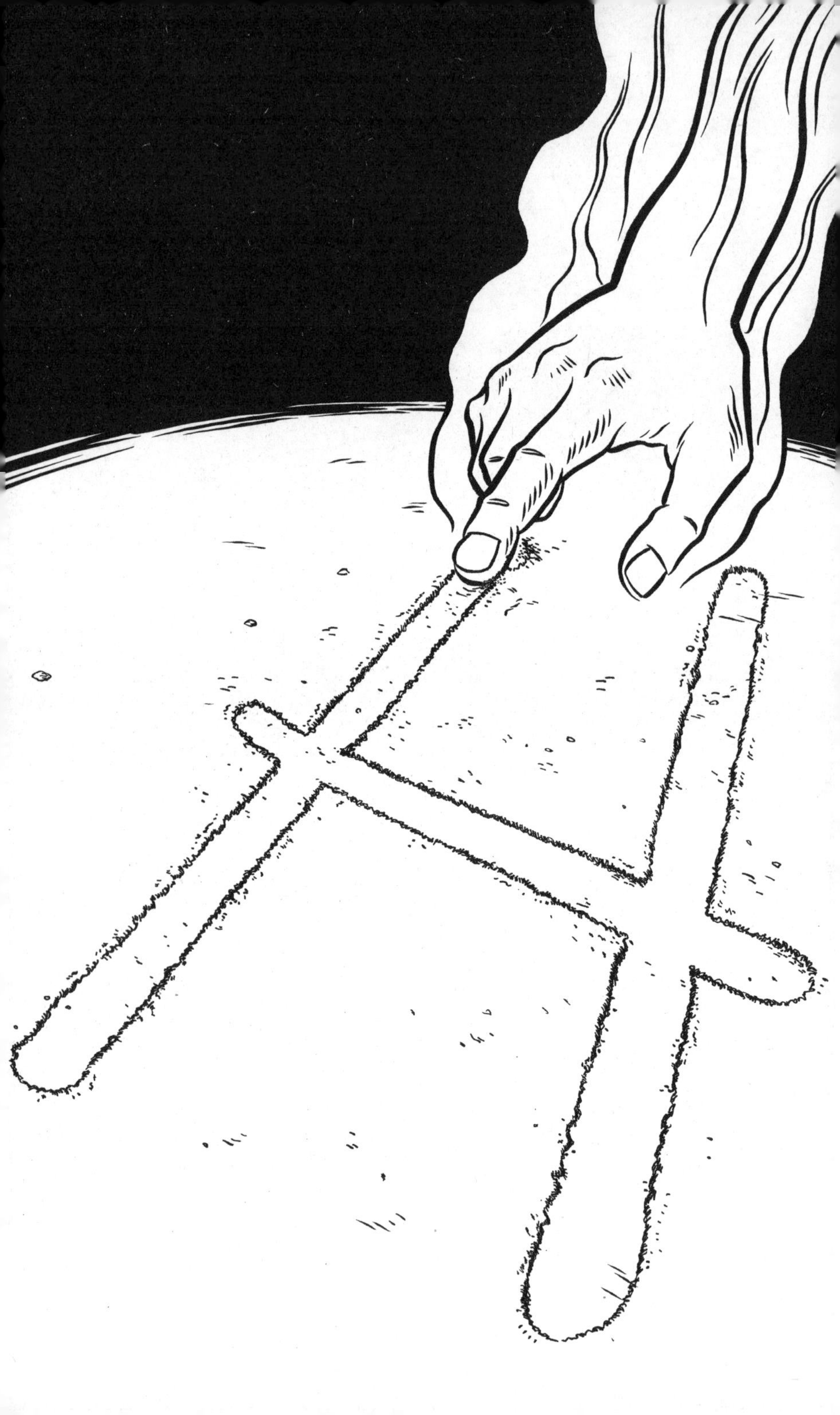

THE POLTERGEIST OF HUMPTY DOO

HUMPTY DOO, AUSTRALIA
1998

In August 1997, Jill Summerville and her partner, Dave Clarke, moved into a rental home in the quiet town of Humpty Doo in Australia's Northern Territory. The house was modest and unassuming and offered them a fresh start in a peaceful environment. Surrounded by the vast Australian landscape, Jill and Dave settled into their new life, and, for a time, everything seemed normal.

In January 1998, their friends Andrew and Kirsty Agius, along with their one-year-old daughter, Jasmine, moved in with them. Almost immediately, objects such as glassware, bottles, and even knives began to launch through the air as if hurled by an unseen force. One particularly disturbing incident involved seashells and gravel inexplicably raining down from the ceiling. The residents were convinced these flying objects were intentionally directed at them, making them feel as though they were under attack.

As the paranormal disturbances escalated, both couples became convinced that an entity was attempting to communicate with them. Their suspicions were confirmed when they discovered Scrabble tiles scattered throughout the house, spelling out words like *fire*, *TV*, *car*, *help*, *no TV*, and *Troy*. The meaning behind these cryptic messages remained a mystery, but their presence only deepened the household's fear.

Soon the activity intensified: Scratching noises echoed from inside the walls, household appliances were mysteriously destroyed, and small piles of stones and gravel materialized throughout the home.

The relentless disturbances left the two couples utterly terrified. Sleep became impossible as they spent their nights awake—crying, shaken, and gripped by an overwhelming sense of dread.

The two couples grew desperate to leave the house, but with nowhere else to go, they found themselves trapped in a nightmare they couldn't escape. Over time, they became skilled at dodging flying objects and began accepting the poltergeist's relentless assaults as part of their daily existence. Then one day, they noticed a trident symbol in their driveway, which had been carefully arranged using small pebbles. This symbol, often associated with demonic entities, pushed the couples to seek help from the church. They could no longer ignore the entity's presence.

They contacted a local priest, Father Stephen de Souza, who arrived with two colleagues to confront the entity head-on. However, the moment they stepped inside, it became clear that whatever lurked within wasn't leaving without a fight. Father de Souza entered first—to a piercing scream of "Father!"—and the moment he turned to respond, a knife resting on the kitchen counter suddenly lifted into the air and hurtled straight toward him. Just as it seemed destined to strike, it stopped mid-flight, as if hitting an invisible barrier, before clattering harmlessly to the floor at his feet.

Bibles were violently snatched from the priests' hands, and when they were later retrieved, pages specifically detailing exorcisms and the casting out of demons were found torn away. Then one of the priests was suddenly grabbed by an unseen force. His arm was wrenched behind his back, and he was thrown to the ground with incredible force, leaving him shaken and in pain.

Rather than subduing the poltergeist, the priests' presence seemed to enrage it further. With the situation growing more dangerous, they called in another priest—Father Tom English. He visited the home four times to help, but he soon concluded that the entity did not obey the known laws of physics. Whatever force they were dealing with was beyond their understanding, and no amount of prayer seemed to weaken its grip.

Father English, lacking experience in dealing with a poltergeist, did what little he could—he blessed the house and sprinkled holy water throughout the rooms, hoping to bring peace to the tormented home. On his final visit, the activity became so intense that he left behind vials of holy water, a crucifix, and a Bible, believing they might offer some protection. But rather than calming the entity, these religious artifacts only seemed to provoke it further. The poltergeist responded with fury, violently flinging the crucifix across the house and spattering the holy water against its walls.

As the supernatural chaos escalated, the entity continued using Scrabble tiles, stones, and gravel to deliver its cryptic messages. The words *Troy*, *fire*, *help*, and *skin* appeared repeatedly, leaving the residents puzzled and unnerved. That was until one of the couples made a chilling connection: The name *Troy* could refer to their close friend, Troy Raddatz, who had tragically died in a fiery car accident just a few miles from the property early that year. This realization only deepened their fears and confusion. They didn't know if the entity was trying to communicate something about their deceased friend or may have actually been Troy trying to communicate from beyond the grave.

As if the relentless and inexplicable paranormal activity wasn't enough, the couples soon faced another problem: their landlord. After stumbling across news of the now-infamous house, the landlord decided to check it out for himself. Seeing that the house was heavily damaged, he decided to take legal action to evict them. However, the judge made an unprecedented ruling that the poltergeist had caused the damage to the home, and therefore the couples could not be held responsible. Despite this unexpected legal victory, it was clear to both couples that they could no longer endure the horrors of the house. Unwilling to spend another night in fear, they made the decision to leave the home behind, hoping to escape the relentless terror that had consumed their lives.

Almost immediately, a new tenant moved into the house, and to everyone's astonishment, the paranormal activity completely ceased. The new resident reported no strange disturbances, no flying objects, no ominous messages—nothing. It was as if the poltergeist had vanished entirely. This led some to believe that the hauntings were specifically tied to Jill, Dave, Andrew, and Kirsty. Had Troy's spirit latched on to them, using the house as a medium to make his presence known? Or was something else, something darker, manipulating their fears? Whether a case of supernatural forces or something yet to be understood, the story of Humpty Doo lingers, a dark and unforgettable chapter in Australia's history of the unexplained.

THE GHOST WHO SOLVED HER OWN MURDER

CHICAGO, ILLINOIS

1977

Amid the bustling streets of Chicago, forty-eight-year-old Teresita Basa was found murdered in her apartment. What initially seemed like a tragic yet ordinary crime ended up being one of the most bizarre and debated investigations in true crime history.

Teresita was born in 1929 in the Philippines, before eventually moving to the United States in the 1960s. At the time, she was married and working as a respiratory therapist at a local hospital. She was also studying for a master's degree in music and giving piano lessons to children in her Chicago neighborhood. Teresita and her husband, Joe, cherished their peaceful existence.

However, on the evening of February 21, 1977, Teresita was inside her Chicago apartment, speaking on the phone with her friend, Ruth Loeb. Their conversation lasted about thirty minutes, and during their chat, Teresita casually mentioned that a man was in her apartment, though she never revealed his name.

An hour after their call ended, neighbors in Teresita's building noticed the strong smell of smoke and quickly alerted the fire department. When firefighters arrived, they searched the building, and upon reaching Teresita's unit, found it locked. After knocking repeatedly with no response, they asked the building's janitor to unlock the door. As they stepped inside, the heavy smoke led them to the bedroom, where they discovered a pile of burning clothes beneath the mattress. As they cleared the debris, they uncovered Teresita's body on the floor, with a knife brutally plunged into her chest.

At first, investigators suspected that Teresita had been sexually assaulted before her murder. However, the medical examiner determined that there was no evidence of sexual assault. With no immediate leads, the case quickly grew cold. For five long months, the police struggled to find any clues or possible motives—Teresita had no known enemies, and those close to her couldn't understand why someone would want her dead.

Then, six months after her murder, Dr. Jose Chua Jr. who worked at the same hospital as Teresita, made a shocking claim—his wife, Remibias, had been experiencing vivid and inexplicable visions about Teresita's murder. One day, Jose witnessed his wife suddenly rise, walk into their bedroom, and lie down on the floor with a vacant, almost lifeless expression on her face. Concerned, he asked what was wrong. But when she replied, the voice that came out was not her own.

The voice coming from his wife spoke in Tagalog but with a distinct Spanish accent—one that Jose, being from the Philippines, immediately recognized. When he asked who was speaking, the voice responded, "Teresita Basa." A chill ran down Jose's spine. His wife—who had no personal connection to the case—appeared to be channeling Teresita's spirit. The voice assured him that there was nothing to fear and began pleading with him to help bring her killer to justice.

After about thirty minutes, Remibias suddenly snapped out of the trance, completely unaware of what had just transpired. Jose, now convinced that his wife had been possessed by Teresita's spirit, was deeply unsettled. Yet, fearing ridicule, he kept the strange incident to himself.

The possessions continued, and Jose remained silent. That was until another trance, the same mysterious voice returned—and this time, it revealed two crucial pieces of information. First, the voice identified Teresita's murderer as Allan Showery, a former coworker. The second startling claim was that after killing Teresita, Allan stole her jewelry and gave it to his girlfriend.

Desperate for answers and wanting justice for Teresita, Jose turned to private investigator Joseph Stachula. He shared with Joseph that he believed Teresita's spirit had possessed his wife to solve her own murder. Intrigued but skeptical, Joseph decided to dig deeper into the case.

While searching Teresita's apartment for overlooked clues, Joseph discovered a note in Teresita's handwriting that read "Get tickets for A. S." Determined to uncover the truth, Joseph investigated further and confirmed that *A. S.* stood for Allan Showery. With this new lead, Joseph, along with investigator Lee Epplen, went to Allan's apartment to question him.

Allan admitted that he knew Teresita, but he initially denied ever being at her apartment on the night of the murder. However, under pressure, he changed his story, claiming that he had, in fact, visited her apartment—but only to fix her television, and he insisted that he left before dark.

Allan's girlfriend, Yanka Kamluk, was questioned next. During her interview, Joseph noticed she was wearing a pearl cocktail ring—one of the items reported stolen from Teresita. When Joseph brought up the missing jewelry, Allan's demeanor changed. Shockingly, he confessed to the murder on the spot. He detailed everything in a thirteen-page confession, admitting that he had gone to Teresita's apartment with the intent to rob her. That night, he was arrested and charged with her murder.

Allan initially attempted to have the case dismissed, arguing that all the evidence against him came from the "great beyond." However, after a mistrial, he ultimately pleaded guilty to Teresita's murder on February 23, 1979. He was sentenced to fourteen years in prison, yet in an unexpected turn of events, he was released on parole in 1983—serving just four years for the brutal crime.

Decades later, this case continues to divide both paranormal believers and true crime enthusiasts, sparking endless debates about what truly happened. The murder of Teresita Basa will forever blur the line between the natural and the supernatural, leaving behind a mystery that may never truly be solved.

THE BLACK MONK OF PONTEFRACT

PONTEFRACT, WEST YORKSHIRE, ENGLAND 1966

When an ordinary family moved into their new home, they were completely unaware of the dark history lurking within its walls. In early 1966, Jean and Joe Pritchard—along with their children, Phillip and Diane—moved into their new home at 30 East Drive, Pontefract, West Yorkshire, England. The family settled in comfortably; however, their peace was short-lived.

That summer, when Phillip was home alone with his grandmother, Sarah Scholes, he noticed a fine layer of chalklike dust falling—not from the ceiling, but from below head height, defying logic. Moments later, puddles of water began forming across the kitchen floor, seemingly from nowhere. Perplexed, Sarah called a plumber, but despite a thorough inspection, no leaks or broken pipes could be found.

That night, Sarah was watching television when she heard Phillip scream from the kitchen. She immediately ran to him, finding tea leaves and sugar scattered all over the countertops. As she tried to process what was in front of her, the tea dispenser started turning on and off on its own, spraying hot tea wildly around the room. Overcome with terror, Sarah screamed, "STOP IT!," hoping to put an end to the madness. Terrified, she grabbed Phillip and fled the house. When they returned later in the night, drawers around the house began violently shaking, rattling as if moved by unseen hands. Feeling uneasy, they decided to stay at a friend's for the night.

When the rest of the Pritchard family returned home, they were immediately met with Sarah's frantic recounting of the unexplainable events, both she and Phillip left shaken. Yet, despite the chaos of that night, the paranormal activity suddenly ceased.

For the next two years, the family lived in peace. But without warning, the disturbances returned with a vengeance, and the house was alive with chaos. Objects were hurled across the house, smashing against walls. The house would drop to freezing cold temperatures, despite the warm weather. Loud, thunderous banging echoed throughout the home at all hours of the day, rattling the walls. Objects vanished, only to reappear in odd locations, as if the entity was taunting them, proving its power. But perhaps the most disturbing was when the Pritchards found their cherished family photographs ravaged, their faces scratched out in a deliberate act of malice.

Eventually, every Pritchard was visited by the entity. At night, the dark figure materialized in their rooms, its form cloaked in shadows. Though its features were obscured, they could see it was draped in a large, loose hood that resembled a monk's robe. The entity loomed silently over the bed, watching them and filling the room with an oppressive, chilling energy. They named the entity "Fred" to make light of the situation and lessen their fear. But behind the humorous name, they all knew Fred was anything but friendly.

Unfortunately, things worsened when the entity made Diane its primary target. On multiple nights, as she lay in bed, the presence forcefully gripped her, yanking her out of bed with terrifying strength. She would suddenly be slapped across the face, jolting her awake in panic and pain. Other times, cold, invisible fingers would wrap around her ankles, yanking her slightly off the bed, just enough to remind her that she was never alone. It seemed Fred thrived on fear, and Diane was his favorite victim. Then, one night, Diane screamed as the entity dragged her up the stairs—its grip so tight that the family found deep, hand-shaped bruises on her neck, undeniable evidence that something malicious had physically attacked her.

Desperate to put an end to Diane's and their family's torment, Jean and Joe reached out to an exorcist and trusted friend, hoping that an exorcism might drive out the malevolent force. But as holy water was sprinkled throughout the house, the entity manifested crosses on the walls, and then one by one, the crosses began to turn upside down, a symbol of defiance and evil.

Then, just as mysteriously as it started, the terrifying encounters, relentless attacks, and mind-bending supernatural events came to a sudden stop. Fred simply vanished, and the house fell silent once again. The Pritchard family eventually moved out of 30 East Drive, leaving its dark memories behind them.

Decades later, disturbing reports continue to emerge as curious onlookers and paranormal investigators frequently visit the infamous house, drawn in by its dark reputation. One particular paranormal investigator, Tom Cuniff, discovered that between 1090 and 1539, a small Cluniac priory once stood mere yards from 30 East Drive. The gallows—where criminals met their gruesome fate—were positioned exactly where the house stood.

Cuniff also uncovered the grim tale of a Cluniac monk who had been found guilty of the rape and murder of a young girl and was ultimately hanged to death—where the Pritchards' home was built centuries later. Disturbingly, the monk's victim had been the same age as Diane Pritchard during her targeted attacks. The family's description of the dark, hooded figure also matched perfectly with the historical accounts of the monk, solidifying the theory that his spirit had never truly left.

Many claim to have seen Fred, or the Black Monk, lurking in the windows of 30 East Drive, watching silently from the darkness within. Investigators have reported strange and aggressive activity, as if their mere presence provokes the entity's wrath. Equipment mysteriously vanishes, objects move on their own, temperatures fluctuate without explanation, and, in one instance, the home was blasted with a suffocating heat. Even after all these years, the Black Monk of Pontefract refuses to fade into obscurity. His dark energy still lingers, terrifying all who dare to step inside 30 East Drive.

THE POLTERGEIST OF FLYING OBJECTS

INDIANAPOLIS, INDIANA
1962

Renate Beck was born in Vienna, Austria. She eventually moved to Indianapolis, Indiana, where she was a local restaurant operator. In early 1962, she had been recently divorced and moved into a large, two-story home with her daughter, Linda, and her mother, Lina Gemmecke. The house was a fresh start: a safe place to raise her daughter, care for her mother, and move forward.

Then on Sunday evening, March 11, 1962, after an ordinary day at the house, things turned chaotic. While in the kitchen around 10:00 p.m., Renate and Lina watched as a beer mug, which had been sitting alone in the sink, was suddenly lifted into the air before crashing to the floor. The two women stood in stunned silence. But their silence didn't last long. Out of nowhere, they heard loud banging and crashing coming from upstairs. Renate, Linda, and Lina immediately feared a home invasion, as their neighborhood had a history of break-ins. But when they cautiously searched the house, no one was there. However, they did find a large piece of German crystal that had flown off a bookshelf, breaking into pieces and landing three or four feet away from where it had been sitting. A bit shaken, they attempted to go about their night. But before long, a heavy glass ashtray was hurled across the room. The air inside the home suddenly felt charged with an unnatural presence. Then, thirty minutes later, another expensive crystal inexplicably shattered.

Overcome with panic, the family made a swift decision to flee, grabbing only what they needed before rushing out the door. They checked into a hotel for the night, hoping that distance would bring them peace. They returned to their home the next afternoon around 1:30 p.m. As they cautiously stepped inside, they were relieved to find that nothing appeared disturbed—there were no new messes, no shattered crystal, and no sign of anything unusual. The house was quiet.

But the silence was short-lived. Within thirty minutes of being home, the shattering returned—even louder and more relentless than before. Glass exploded, sending sharp shards across the floor. Frantic, they rushed from room to room, only to find their home in complete disarray. Bowls, vases, and glassware had been violently thrown from their places, now lying scattered, broken, and cracked across nearly every surface.

Then, just as Lina rose from her chair, a coffee cup, which had been sitting in the sink on the other side of the room, launched itself at an unnatural speed, smashing into the wall just inches above where she had been sitting. If she hadn't moved, the cup would have struck her head directly. It was no coincidence—whatever was in the house was aware of them, watching them, and reacting to their movements. At this point, Renate, Linda, and Lina could no longer deny the truth—something deeply disturbing was going on in their home. They did the only thing that seemed logical—they called the police.

Sergeant John Mullin was the first officer to arrive on the scene. As he stepped inside, he was immediately struck by how visibly shaken Renate, Linda, and Lina appeared—their nerves on edge, their hands trembling. The house itself bore the evidence of their terror—glass, plates, and shattered objects littered the floors, turning their home into what looked like the aftermath of a violent break-in or attack. But there was no intruder and no signs of forced entry. Sergeant Mullin initially speculated that the damage had been caused by a pellet gun, a theory that didn't hold up given the house's intact storm windows. There was simply no way for an external force to fire anything inside. As more officers arrived to investigate, the disturbances showed no signs of stopping.

Patrolman Ray Patton was making his way through the house when he heard a sudden crash in Linda's bedroom. Startled but curious, he quickly ascended the stairs and entered the room, only to discover a shattered glass swan in the center of the floor. The delicate figure had been sitting on a shelf, and there was no one around who could have knocked it over. Several other officers searching the house brought in high-frequency sound equipment, hoping to find a rational explanation. As they searched and conducted their tests inside, the outside of the house had become a spectacle. Word of the paranormal activity had spread like wildfire, drawing hundreds of curious onlookers to the Becks' home. People crowded the sidewalks, whispering, their eyes fixed on the house, hoping to glimpse something inexplicable.

During all the commotion, Renate's purse, which contained $125, mysteriously vanished. Police conducted an exhaustive search of the house, turning over every possible hiding place, but the purse was nowhere to be found. Soon after, Renate and Linda found bite marks on their hands and arms, with no clue where they came from. There were some officers who theorized that bats were responsible, but it was unlikely that bats would be flying inside, in the middle of an Indiana winter.

By the end of the day, the violent disturbances had largely ceased, but the house itself looked as though a hurricane had torn through it. Shattered mirrors, broken glass, and fragments of pottery littered the floors. Feathers from ripped pillows floated through the air, picture frames had been torn apart, and the walls were scarred with deep dents from the countless objects that had been hurled against them.

On March 25th, fourteen days after the initial activity, Renate's missing purse inexplicably reappeared. The police were informed, and when they arrived at the home the next day, they found Lina lying on the floor, dazed and semiconscious. Then, in front of one of the officers, she suddenly hurled a heavy glass ashtray across the room and even overturned a piano. Given the violent and similar nature of the recent events, officers immediately placed her under arrest, suspecting that she had been responsible for the chaos all along. Renate insisted that her mother needed medical care, so Lina was taken to the hospital for evaluation before being placed in the city jail overnight. In court the next day, the judge suggested a mental examination but agreed to drop the case if Lina returned to Germany, her home country, within ten days. Lina accepted the deal and was released into Renate's care.

The media quickly twisted the story, claiming that the strange activity in the house wasn't a supernatural entity—it was Lina Gemmecke herself. Lieutenant Francis Dux later visited the family, attempting to provoke the so-called poltergeist. He gathered everyone in one room for an hour and a half, watching for any signs of activity. When nothing happened, he concluded that the disturbances only occurred when at least one family member was out of sight. Based on his brief observation, he dismissed the case entirely. However, a family friend, Emil Noseda, who was present for all sixteen days of the haunting, strongly disagreed. He had personally witnessed objects flying, furniture moving, and unexplainable disturbances. He also asserted that the activity had already stopped before Lina's arrest, proving that whatever had tormented the family had nothing to do with her.

To this day, no one knows for certain whether the events at the Becks' home were due to emotional explosions, an elaborate hoax, or the work of a true poltergeist. Whatever happened in that house left a lasting mark—not just on the family, but on Indiana's map of supernatural legend.

CHAPTER TWO

THE GONE

Abductions, Missing Persons, and Kidnappings

GONE IN THE NIGHT

SHELBY, NORTH CAROLINA
2000

In the predawn hours of February 14, 2000, nine-year-old Asha Degree quietly packed her backpack, slipped out of her family's home in Shelby, North Carolina, and ventured into the darkness alone. Around 4:00 a.m., she was spotted walking along Highway 18 in the middle of a powerful rainstorm, a thin figure barely visible against the night. A passing motorist, concerned for the young girl's safety, slowed down and attempted to approach her—but before they could help, Asha bolted into the nearby woods and vanished. She was never seen again.

Born on August 5, 1990, in Shelby, North Carolina, Asha was raised in a loving and structured home by her parents, Harold and Iquilla Degree. She grew up alongside her brother, O'Bryant, who was just a year older. The siblings were close. They rarely strayed far from home and were always truthful. Asha was known for her shy and sensible nature—she was the kind of child who never acted without her parents' approval, making her disappearance all the more baffling.

Her parents were protective, ensuring their children weren't heavily influenced by outside pressures. At the time, Asha was a fourth grader, and her school was heading into a three-day weekend. On Friday, February 11, classes were canceled, so she and O'Bryant spent the day at their aunt's house until their parents returned from work. The following day, Asha played in a basketball game as one of her team's star players, but for the first time that season, they lost.

Sunday, February 13, was a typical day. The family attended church before returning home and settling into their nightly routine. Asha and O'Bryant went to bed around 8:00 p.m. in their shared bedroom.

Throughout the night, Harold checked on his children multiple times, each time finding them asleep. He finally went to bed around 2:00 a.m. The next morning, Asha was gone.

When Iquilla went to wake Asha for school the next morning and found her bed empty, she immediately knew something was wrong. Panicked, she searched the house, but Asha was nowhere to be found. When they questioned O'Bryant, he recalled hearing the faint squeak of Asha's bed in the middle of the night, but he had assumed she was just shifting in her sleep.

The family immediately contacted the police, and officers arrived at the scene to find no signs of forced entry. A closer inspection of Asha's belongings revealed that she had packed a backpack in advance, filling it with several sets of clothes and personal items—an indication that she had left the house voluntarily. However, where she had gone and why remained a mystery.

With no immediate leads, canine units were brought in, but they failed to pick up Asha's scent. Just when it seemed like the trail had gone cold, investigators received their first major clue: A truck driver and a motorist both reported seeing a young girl, matching Asha's description, walking alone along Highway 18 around 4:00 a.m. One of the witnesses found it odd that such a young girl was out alone at that hour, especially in the middle of a raging storm. Concerned, he turned his vehicle around to check on her, but as he approached, the girl suddenly darted off the highway and disappeared into the dense woods. That was the last confirmed sighting of Asha.

The following day, investigators found Asha's hair bow, along with a candy wrapper, a pencil, and a green marker, inside a nearby shed. Determined to find more evidence, authorities launched a massive search effort, enlisting nine thousand volunteers to scour a two- to three-mile radius for an entire week. Despite their efforts, nothing else was found. In the days that followed, investigators received roughly three hundred tips, but none led to any breakthroughs. Asha had seemingly vanished.

At this point, the FBI and North Carolina State Bureau of Investigation joined the search efforts, bringing in additional resources and expertise to help locate Asha. Meanwhile, her devastated family refused to give up hope. Determined to keep her name in the public eye, they made numerous television appearances, speaking about her case on national platforms such as *The Montel Williams Show* and *The Oprah Winfrey Show*. They pleaded for answers, hoping that someone, somewhere, might know something that could bring their daughter home.

Unfortunately, they waited nearly a year and a half before construction workers stumbled upon Asha's backpack—thirty miles from where she was last seen. Inside the backpack were a few of Asha's belongings, including her New Kids on the Block T-shirt and a copy of Dr. Seuss's *McElligot's Pool*. The investigators closely examined Asha's backpack and its contents, as well as thoroughly searching the surrounding area. However, their work yielded no further clues as to what happened to Asha.

In 2004, about three years after finding Asha's backpack, investigators received a new lead. A prison inmate claimed Asha had been murdered and that he knew her burial site. Authorities took the tip seriously and began an excavation at the location he provided. But their hopes were shattered when the remains they uncovered turned out to be nothing more than animal bones. Another dead end.

Despite repeated setbacks, the Degree family refused to let their daughter's case be forgotten, making it their mission to keep Asha's memory alive. They put up giant billboards, established a scholarship in Asha's name, and founded an annual walk from their home to Highway 18, where she was last seen. Year after year, they have continued to fight for answers, clinging to the hope that one day, Asha will come home.

Over the years, countless tips have come in, but every lead has either gone cold or led to a dead end, leaving Asha's case shrouded in unanswered questions and lingering uncertainty. Cleveland County Detective Tim Adams continues to hold on to hope, believing that someone, somewhere, knows the truth about her disappearance. Despite exhaustive searches conducted by thousands of volunteers, law enforcement agencies, and even the FBI, no further trace of Asha—no remains, no confirmed sightings—has ever been found.

The pain of not knowing has weighed heavily on Asha's family for over two decades. The National Center for Missing and Exploited Children has released multiple digitally age-progressed images over the years, with the most recent one depicting what Asha might look like at thirty years old. Seeing the image was bittersweet for her mother, Iquilla Degree, who still clings to hope but grapples with the agony of uncertainty. "This is worse than death," she once said in an interview. "Because at least with death, you have closure. You can go to a gravesite, or if you have the urn at home. But for us, we can't mourn, we can't give up. The only thing we got is hope."

Despite the relentless efforts of investigators, journalists, her family, and her community, Asha remains lost to the world.

THE BAR THAT SWALLOWED BRIAN SHAFFER

COLUMBUS, OHIO
2006

Brian Randall Shaffer was born on February 25, 1979, in Ohio. He was known as a fun-loving, responsible, and intelligent young man, excelling both academically and socially. After graduating from high school, he set his sights on The Ohio State University (OSU), where he began studying medicine in 2004. But while Brian was dedicated to his studies, his true passion lay elsewhere—deep down, he dreamed of starting his own band. He loved the exhilarating, fast-paced lifestyle of musicians and often talked about how thrilling it would be to pursue that path instead.

Sadly, Brian's life took a tragic turn during his second year at OSU when his mother, Renee Shaffer, passed away from cancer. Although he outwardly seemed to handle the loss well, those closest to him knew it had affected him deeply. Despite the pain, Brian found comfort in his relationship with Alexis Waggoner, a fellow medical student. Their relationship was strong, filled with love and support, and those around them were convinced that Brian was preparing to take the next step. In fact, many believed he was planning to propose to Alexis during their upcoming spring break trip to Miami.

On March 31, 2006, just as spring break was beginning, Brian had dinner with his father, Randy Shaffer. His father noticed that Brian seemed exhausted, most likely from the long hours he had spent preparing for his upcoming exams. Concerned, Randy thought Brian should take it easy that night, but he chose not to say anything.

Brian, however, had already made plans to go out with his roommate, William "Clint" Florence. That night, Brian and William headed to the Ugly Tuna Saloona, a popular bar near The Ohio State University, looking to unwind after weeks of grueling study sessions for their upcoming finals. At around 10:00 p.m., Brian took a moment to call Alexis, expressing how much he loved her and how excited he was for their upcoming spring break trip to Miami, which was just a couple of days away.

After the call, Brian and William moved from bar to bar, taking shots of hard liquor at each stop, letting loose as the night unfolded. Eventually, they made their way to the Arena District, where they met up with William's friend Meredith Reed. After a few more drinks, the three decided to return to where the night began—the Ugly Tuna Saloona. At approximately 1:15 a.m., security cameras captured them riding the escalator up to the bar's second floor. Then, at around 2:00 a.m., security footage showed Brian outside the bar—without his friends—talking to two women. After a brief conversation, he said goodbye, and without any sign of distress, he reentered the bar. That would be the last time Brian Shaffer was ever seen.

As the bar began closing for the night, William and Meredith realized Brian was nowhere to be found. They called his phone multiple times, but he never answered. Concerned, they waited outside, carefully watching as every person left the bar, hoping to spot Brian in the crowd. But he never came out. Confused, they assumed he had left without telling them and returned to his apartment alone.

By the next morning, Brian was still unreachable. All weekend, William and Brian's father repeatedly tried calling him, but their calls went straight to voicemail. Then came Monday—the day of his long-awaited Miami trip with Alexis. When Brian didn't show up for his flight, it became clear that something was terribly wrong, so his loved ones reported him missing to the Columbus police.

In the days following Brian's disappearance, law enforcement launched an extensive search effort. At any given time, at least fifty police officers were actively looking for him. Search dogs were deployed, sniffing through alleys, dumpsters, and even abandoned buildings. Officers questioned local residents and business owners, asking if they had seen or heard anything unusual. Despite their exhaustive efforts, they found nothing—no trace of Brian, no evidence of foul play, and no personal belongings left behind.

Additionally, investigators thoroughly questioned Brian's family and friends, all of whom cooperated and passed polygraph tests—except for one notable exception: his roommate, William Florence. The two women Brian was last seen speaking with outside the Ugly Tuna Saloona were never interviewed by authorities.

Officers also reviewed hours of surveillance footage from the Ugly Tuna Saloona, but the cameras failed to catch him leaving. Investigators considered several possibilities: Could he have disguised himself by changing clothes, wearing a hat, and keeping his head down to avoid detection? Could he have slipped out through an alternate exit? The police decided to expand their search, reviewing surveillance footage from surrounding businesses, hoping to catch a glimpse of Brian somewhere outside the bar. But there was no sign of him anywhere.

As the investigation stalled, police started to explore alternative theories beyond an accident or an abduction. One possibility was that Brian had willingly disappeared, perhaps as a way to grieve in solitude following his mother's recent death. But his family dismissed this theory outright, saying that Brian had no reason to run away—he had so much to look forward to. He was about to go on a long-planned trip with his girlfriend to Miami, where many believed he was going to propose to her.

Alexis, devastated and desperate for answers, called Brian's cell phone every night before going to sleep. Each time, it went straight to voicemail—until one night, when the phone rang three times before disconnecting. Her heart leaped at the possibility that Brian was alive and that someone, somewhere, had his phone. However, when authorities investigated, the wireless provider dismissed it as nothing more than a technical glitch.

Despite hundreds of tips pouring in, none led to a breakthrough in the case. One theory suggested that Brian had fallen victim to the so-called "Smiley Face Killer," a rumored serial killer who left smiley-face graffiti at his crime scenes and was allegedly responsible for the deaths of numerous young men across the country. However, no concrete evidence ever linked his disappearance to this theory.

After a year, hope for Brian's return began to fade. His credit cards remained untouched, his bank account showed no activity, and his cell phone was never used again. With no new leads and no evidence of Brian's whereabouts, the case gradually faded from the public eye.

Brian's father, Randy, struggled to accept his son's grim reality, so he kept searching. Tragically, Randy died in 2008, when a tree fell down and fatally struck him during a windstorm. Randy's death left Brian's younger brother, Derek, as the only surviving member of the Shaffer family. Despite the passage of time, Derek has never given up searching for his brother, still hoping for answers to the mystery that has haunted him.

In 2020, a glimmer of hope emerged when a photograph surfaced online of an unhoused American man living in Mexico. The man bore a striking resemblance to Brian, igniting widespread speculation that he had finally been found. The FBI conducted an extensive facial recognition analysis, but after thorough testing, they determined the man was not Brian Shaffer. It was yet another devastating dead end.

To this day, one question remains: How can someone enter a building and simply vanish into thin air?

THE ESCAPE OF JAYME CLOSS

BARRON, WISCONSIN
2018

The Closs family, consisting of parents James and Denise, along with their thirteen-year-old daughter Jayme, lived in the small town of Barron, Wisconsin. Jayme had a typical teenage life: She loved hanging out with her friends, dancing, and going to school. Unfortunately, one day while stepping onto the school bus, she unknowingly caught the attention of twenty-one-year-old Jake Patterson. For Patterson, a dark and twisted obsession immediately took hold—he knew Jayme was the girl he wanted to take.

Over the next few days, Patterson drove to Jayme's home twice, intending to abduct her. But each time, he backed out, spooked by cars in the driveway or movement inside the house. However, on his third attempt, October 15, 2018, he came armed with a shotgun, ready to do anything.

Patterson parked his car at the end of the driveway, dressed in a black coat and ski mask. As he approached the front door, the Closs family's dog began barking loudly. Jayme's father, James, heard the disturbance and got up to investigate. Peering through the window with a flashlight, he demanded to know who was outside. Instead of answering, Patterson screamed, "OPEN THE FUCKING DOOR!"

When James refused, Patterson raised his shotgun and fired through the window, killing James instantly. Patterson forced his way in and began methodically searching each room, determined to get Jayme and willing to hurt anyone in his way. Denise, hearing the gunshot, grabbed Jayme and frantically called 911 before hiding in the bathroom. Patterson eventually found the locked bathroom and began pounding on it relentlessly. When he finally broke in, he found Denise clutching her terrified daughter, who was hysterically crying.

Patterson grabbed Jayme, bound her wrists and ankles, and forced Denise to put duct tape over Jayme's mouth—only to raise his shotgun and kill Denise right in front of her daughter.

As Patterson carried Jayme out of the house, he nearly slipped in the pool of blood left by her father. He shoved her into the trunk of his car and sped away. The entire ordeal—from the moment he entered the house to the moment he fled—took only four minutes.

Meanwhile, the 911 dispatcher who received Denise's panicked call and heard screaming in the background had immediately sent officers to the scene. As Patterson drove away, barely twenty seconds from the house, flashing police lights whizzed past him in the opposite direction. But they paid him no attention.

When officers arrived at the Closs home, they were met with sheer horror. James and Denise were dead, their blood staining the floors. But something was missing—there was no sign of Jayme. Investigators quickly ruled her out as a suspect and issued an Amber Alert.

Unfazed by the chaos he left behind, Patterson then drove seventy miles to his secluded cabin in Gordon, Wisconsin. His first act upon arrival was to destroy evidence—he burned Jayme's clothes and warned her that if she made any noise or tried to escape, he would kill her, just like he had killed her parents.

Jayme was now his prisoner, and his methods of imprisonment were cruel and calculated. Whenever he left the house, he forced Jayme under his small twin-size bed, barricading it with storage boxes and placing heavy barbells on top to ensure she couldn't escape. Sometimes she would remain trapped there for up to twelve hours at a time, with no food, water, or access to a bathroom.

She was forced to sleep beside him in his bed and was only allowed outside for brief walks—always after Patterson thoroughly checked to make sure no one was around.

As time passed, Patterson became more confident that Jayme was too terrified to escape. He stopped taking extra precautions, trusting that his threats had completely broken her spirit. He allowed her more freedom inside the house, and over time, they settled into a twisted routine. They watched TV together, played board games, and even cooked meals side by side. But beneath Jayme's quiet compliance, she was carefully observing Patterson, waiting for the perfect moment to make her move.

For nearly three months, she endured captivity—isolated from the world, trapped with the man who had brutally murdered her parents and stolen her life. Then, on January 10, 2019, Jayme finally saw her chance. That day, Patterson told her he would be gone for a few hours. As usual, he forced her under his bed, blocking her in with heavy storage bins and weights. But this time, as soon as she heard his car drive away, she shoved aside the barriers that had trapped her for months. She grabbed a pair of Patterson's oversize shoes, flung open the door, and sprinted into the cold Wisconsin air, desperate to find help.

After running down the snow-covered road, Jayme spotted a woman walking her dog. She sprinted toward her, gasping for breath. The woman, Jeanne Nutter, instantly recognized Jayme and, without hesitation, led her to a nearby neighbor's house. Inside, they locked the doors, wrapped Jayme in warm blankets, and called 911. As they waited for police to arrive, Jayme described who had taken her and where she had been held. The neighbors listened to the awful details and comforted Jayme as best they could while they waited for help.

Meanwhile, Patterson returned home and immediately sensed something was wrong. He rushed inside and found the barricade broken wide open. Realizing Jayme had escaped, he jumped into his car and began searching for her, but it was already too late.

As police transported Jayme to the hospital, they spotted Patterson's car on the opposite side of the road, immediately turned around, and pulled him over. Patterson surrendered without resistance and confessed to everything. Later in court, he pleaded guilty to two counts of first-degree murder and the kidnapping of Jayme Closs. The judge sentenced him to two consecutive life sentences without the possibility of parole—plus an additional forty years for the kidnapping.

After eighty-eight grueling days in captivity, Jayme had reclaimed her freedom. She moved in with her aunt, where she was surrounded by the love and support of her remaining family. She was even reunited with her dog. Jayme returned to the life she loved, rejoining her favorite school activities and immersing herself in dance. She worked hard to reclaim the childhood that had been so cruelly stolen from her. Though the scars of her ordeal would never fully fade, she refused to let fear—or her past—dictate her future. Over time, she became an advocate for missing and exploited children, using her story to spread awareness and inspire others to never lose hope.

SEVEN YEARS IN A BOX

EUGENE, OREGON

1977

Colleen Stan set out on a hitchhiking journey from Eugene, Oregon, to Northern California. At twenty years old, she considered herself an experienced hitchhiker, someone who knew how to trust her instincts and stay safe. She had already turned down two rides, sensing something off about the drivers. But when a blue van pulled up beside her, carrying a seemingly harmless couple with a baby aboard, her worries eased. A man, his wife, and their child—surely they weren't dangerous.

The young couple, Cameron and Janice Hooker, seemed quite ordinary, but when they stopped at a gas station along the way, Colleen suddenly felt an unshakable sense of dread creep over her. A voice in her head urged her to run, to escape while she still had the chance. But she dismissed it, convincing herself she was overreacting. With a deep breath, she walked back to the van and climbed inside.

After about twenty minutes on the road, Cameron suddenly veered off the highway, claiming he wanted to explore some nearby caves. Janice got out with the baby and walked toward a nearby lake. Colleen barely had time to react before Cameron lunged at her, pressing a knife to her throat. Then he tied Colleen up and forced her into a headbox—a twenty-pound wooden device designed to completely enclose her head, blocking out light, sound, and even restricting airflow. Trapped in suffocating darkness, Colleen had no idea that this was only the beginning of her torment.

For years, Cameron had been forcing his violent bondage fantasies upon Janice. Looking for a way out, she struck a desperate agreement with her husband—he could find another woman to take her place. He chose Colleen Stan.

After what felt like an eternity, the van finally arrived at the Hookers' home. Cameron dragged Colleen into the basement and suspended her from the ceiling by her wrists, restraining her and painfully stretching her arms.

Then Cameron tormented Colleen by beating, burning, electrocuting, and whipping her body—every scream met with indifference. When the brutal session ended, Cameron and Janice blindfolded her and left her hanging, her body throbbing in agony. She was then forced to listen as the couple engaged in sex beneath her because Janice had one rule: no intercourse with Colleen.

They also forced her to sign a contract, legally binding her to them. Colleen had no choice but to comply.

After about six months, the Hookers moved into a mobile home. There, Colleen was confined to a coffin-like wooden box, tucked beneath the couple's bed, for up to twenty-three hours a day. The air was stale; the space was too tight to move—her world had been reduced to darkness. The Hookers now had two young children who lived in the same home, completely unaware that a woman was being held captive just inches away from where they slept.

For the small sliver of time she was allowed out, Colleen was forced to clean the house and babysit the children. She was stripped of her name, now referred to only as "K," and commanded to address Cameron as "Master." Cameron also grew tired of his restrictions, but instead of breaking their no-sex deal outright, he found loopholes—he orally raped Colleen and used disturbing instruments on her, satisfying his sadistic urges.

Despite the relentless physical, sexual, and psychological abuse, Colleen's greatest fear was The Company, an all-seeing, all-knowing, powerful satanic cult—and Cameron was a devout member. According to Cameron, The Company had her family's home bugged and monitored her every move, and if she ever tried to escape or disobey him, they would kill her loved ones without hesitation. Cameron's manipulation tactic worked, and even when Colleen was left alone with an open door, a working telephone, and neighbors just a few feet away, she never dared to make a move—her fear of The Company was stronger than her will to run.

Over the years, as Colleen became more obedient to Cameron's demands, he started granting her more freedoms and thereby created an illusion of normalcy. She was allowed to work in the garden, go on jogs, get a job at a local hotel, and, shockingly, even visit her family. But there was always a catch. When she visited, Cameron was right by her side, introducing himself as her loving boyfriend. Colleen, brainwashed and afraid for her family's safety, never breathed a word about her captivity.

Colleen's family, though relieved to see her, sensed something was off. Her appearance, strange behavior, and distant demeanor led them to believe she was involved in a cult. Yet, rather than pressuring her for answers, they chose to tread lightly, afraid that if they questioned her too much, she might disappear again.

Cameron's growing sense of power led him to a disturbing new demand—he wanted Colleen to become his second wife. This was a turning point for Janice, who had tolerated Cameron's wishes and demands for years. For the first time, she started questioning everything that she and Colleen had endured. Janice, realizing that she too had been brainwashed and tortured by Cameron for years, confessed to Colleen that Cameron wasn't a member of The Company, and that he only said that to keep her obedient.

Colleen saw an opportunity for freedom. With Janice's help, she escaped to a bus station, her heart pounding as she made a life-changing phone call. When Cameron answered, Colleen told him she was leaving. His response was unexpected—he broke down in tears. The man who had controlled her every move, who had treated her as an object, was suddenly powerless. Colleen boarded the bus and returned home, finally leaving the nightmare behind.

Colleen didn't immediately go to the police. She even continued to call Cameron in the following months, believing that, at Janice's request, he could change. Three months later, Janice reported Cameron to the police and in a 1985 trial testified against her husband in exchange for full immunity. Her testimony painted a harrowing picture of the years of abuse she and Colleen had suffered. In the end, Cameron Hooker was sentenced to 104 years in prison for kidnapping, torture, and sexual assault, ensuring he would never be able to harm another woman again. Both Colleen and Janice changed their names and continued living in California. However, despite once sharing a bond forged in trauma, they no longer speak.

Colleen endured unimaginable physical and psychological torment—and still does to this day. Despite everything, she rebuilt her life—eventually marrying and having a daughter.

THE FROG BOYS OF SOUTH KOREA

DAEGU, SOUTH KOREA

1991

Five boys—Woo Cheol-won, thirteen, Jo Ho-yeon, twelve, Kim Yeong-gyu, eleven, Park Chan-in, ten, and Kim Jong-sik, ten—set out to catch frogs in the streams of Mount Waryong, South Korea, on their day off from school. It wasn't unusual for the boys to stay out all day, but when the sun started setting and there was no sign of them, their parents grew worried. As the hours kept passing, worry turned into panic. The families scoured the area, calling out the boys' names, but there was no trace of them. Desperate, they called the police and reported them missing.

All five families lived in the same small village, their homes forming a close-knit circle. The boys spent nearly every day together and were described by many as inseparable—closer than brothers. They were known as the "Five Musketeers." Their disappearance sent shock waves through the country, triggering an all-out effort to bring them home. Millions of flyers flooded the streets, and their faces were printed on milk cartons, billboards, candy wrappers, and even animated cartoons. The nation dubbed them the "Frog Boys."

When the case gained national attention, South Korea's president at the time, Roh Tae-woo, ordered an unprecedented search effort. A staggering 300,000 people—including military personnel, police, and volunteers—combed through reservoirs, waterways, bus terminals, and train stations across the country. Despite their efforts, there were no clues or sightings—nothing to suggest what had happened.

On top of that, over five hundred leads flooded in, but every single one was a dead end. To make matters worse, hoaxers began taking advantage of the case, claiming to have the children and demanding ransom money. The boys' parents and police followed these tips, only to find empty locations—and their hopes shattered. Theories ran wild, too. Some believed the boys had been abducted by a mentally ill person, while others suggested they had simply run away. But deep down, the parents knew something terrible had happened. And they refused to give up.

The fathers of all five children quit their jobs to devote themselves entirely to the search. Kim Yeong-gyu's father barely allowed himself to sleep, haunted by dreams of his son, only to wake up and face the same devastating reality—his child was still missing.

As days turned into weeks, then months, then years, investigators were no closer to solving the case. The boys' families were consumed by grief and started turning on one another—blaming each other for not keeping a close enough watch on the children that day.

Then, on September 26, 2002—eleven years after the boys' disappearance—two men hiking on Mount Waryong stumbled upon human remains, just a mile from where the boys had lived. The hikers called the authorities, and soon, family members arrived to confirm the unthinkable. The Frog Boys had finally been found. Their bodies had deteriorated to bones, their clothing tattered and buried with them.

At first, investigators theorized that the boys had tragically frozen to death, victims of exposure rather than violence. But when forensic experts conducted autopsies, they uncovered evidence that all five boys had been brutally murdered. Several of the boys had suffered severe head trauma, either from blunt force injuries or gunshot wounds. One of the skulls had two bullet holes, while others bore strange markings etched into the bone. These gruesome findings made it clear that their deaths were no accident—but it didn't explain how their bodies had gone undiscovered for more than a decade, especially when they were discovered so close to their homes.

Forensic experts studied the boys' remains and, from the moss growth on their skulls, confirmed they had not been moved in years. The boys had died around the time of their disappearance in 1991, meaning their killer had left them undisturbed for over a decade. Pieces of the boys' clothing had also been tied together in an unusual knot, leading authorities to theorize that their killer may have had experience in an industrial or military setting, someone familiar with binding or restraining techniques.

In 2006, the statute of limitations for the case officially expired, seemingly closing the door on any future prosecution. The families of the victims were left with nothing but questions and heartbreak, forced to accept that their children's killer might never be brought to justice. However, in 2015, South Korea's National Assembly abolished the statute of limitations for first-degree murder, reigniting hope that if a suspect were ever identified, they could still face the consequences of their actions.

Yet, despite this legal change, the Frog Boys case remains unresolved. More than three decades later, their families, the investigators, and the nation of South Korea are still left wondering: Who killed these five innocent children, and why?

MISSING
JOHNNY GOSCH
DATE MISSING: 9/5/82
FROM W. DES MOINES, 1A
DOB 11/12/69
WHITE MALE
EYES: Blue
HEIGHT: 5'7"
WEIGHT: 140
HAIR: Brown
milk

THE MILK CARTON KIDNAPPING

WEST DES MOINES, IOWA
1982

In the early morning hours of September 5, 1982, twelve-year-old Johnny Gosch set out on his usual newspaper delivery route in West Des Moines, Iowa, accompanied by his dog. His father, John Gosch, usually joined him but decided to stay home. Around 7:45 a.m., John and Noreen Gosch received a phone call from an irritated neighbor who wanted to know why his newspaper hadn't been delivered yet. John and Noreen were instantly alarmed. Johnny was always punctual, and by that time, he should have been home. Their concern deepened when, a short while later, the family's dog returned home alone—without Johnny. John rushed outside to search for his son. As he scoured the neighborhood, his heart sank when he came across Johnny's small red wagon, still filled with neatly stacked newspapers. There was no sign of his son.

John and Noreen immediately contacted the police. However, the authorities were dismissive, citing the lack of a ransom note or any clear signs of abduction. Instead, they speculated that Johnny had run away and, following standard procedure at the time, refused to initiate a search until seventy-two hours had passed—losing critical hours for Johnny and his family.

When law enforcement finally began investigating, they spoke with several local paperboys who were out that morning and each recalled seeing Johnny speaking with a man in a blue Ford around 6 a.m. One boy remembered seeing a man trail Johnny in his car as Johnny walked a block north from where his route began. Another fellow paperboy, Mike, along with several other witnesses, observed the man eventually shut off his car engine and open the passenger door near the area where the boys would prepare their newspapers. The stranger then asked Johnny for directions, and after a brief exchange, Johnny turned to walk away. John Rossi, who happened to be nearby, also noticed the interaction and immediately sensed something was off. Though he couldn't have known it at the time, Rossi was likely the last person to see Johnny.

According to additional reports, the man in the blue Ford restarted his engine and flashed his headlights three times—an action that many believe was a signal for another person. Almost immediately, a figure emerged from between the houses and began following Johnny. However, these accounts did not lead to any new suspects.

Determined to find their son, John and Noreen launched an exhaustive awareness campaign. They distributed more than ten thousand posters featuring Johnny's face, plastering them throughout their community and beyond. They also made several televised appearances, pleading for any information that could help bring their son home. Despite their efforts, no one came forward with useful information to find Johnny.

Two years later, tragedy struck again. Another paperboy, thirteen-year-old Eugene Martin, vanished under almost identical circumstances—this time only twelve miles from where Johnny went missing. Eugene's disappearance reignited public concern about Johnny's disappearance and fueled growing fears that a predator was targeting young paperboys in the area.

A relative of Eugene worked at a local dairy business and suggested using milk cartons to help spread awareness. The company immediately agreed, printing Johnny's and Eugene's faces on their cartons in hopes of reaching someone who knew the truth.

For years after Johnny vanished, sightings surfaced across the country. In 1983, a woman in Tulsa, Oklahoma, claimed to have encountered a boy who matched Johnny's description. He sprinted up to her in a public place, his face frantic, and gasped, "Please, lady, help me. My name is Johnny Gosch." Before she could process what was happening, two men appeared out of nowhere, grabbed the boy, and dragged him away into the crowd.

The woman was left stunned, her story dismissed by many as a case of mistaken identity or an overactive imagination. Two years later, in 1985, a woman in Iowa received a dollar bill as change at a grocery store. When she looked closer, she noticed something scrawled on the bill: "I am Alive," followed by what appeared to be Johnny's signature. The handwriting was later analyzed and confirmed to be his, reigniting hope—and fear—about his fate.

But the most bizarre account came from Johnny's own mother, Noreen. In March 1997, at around 2:30 a.m., she was awakened by a knock on the door. When she opened the door, she found a stranger, along with a man she immediately recognized as her son—now twenty-seven years old—standing on her doorstep. She claimed that Johnny opened his shirt to reveal a birthmark, a detail only she would know, confirming his identity. Then, Johnny and the man stepped inside, and for over an hour, they spoke in hushed tones. She also noticed that Johnny was constantly glancing over at the man, as if seeking his permission to talk. Johnny warned her not to contact the police, insisting that doing so would put both their lives in danger.

Noreen claimed Johnny told her he had been kidnapped and sold into a child sex trafficking ring. Noreen's story was met with skepticism, even from Johnny's father, John. Many dismissed her account as the desperate imaginings of a grieving mother, but she knew it had happened. Then, almost a decade later, in 2006, a mysterious package arrived at her home. Inside were three photographs that depicted several boys who were bound and gagged. One of the boys bore an unmistakable resemblance to Johnny, and Noreen was convinced it was her son. The police, however, dismissed the photos, claiming they were staged by a group of friends playing a prank. Noreen refused to believe this explanation. To her, the boy in the photo was Johnny, and no one could shake her conviction.

Her confidence was further fueled by Paul Bonacci, a man serving time in prison for sexually assaulting a child. Bonacci claimed he had been kidnapped as a child and forced into a sex trafficking ring and was later coerced into participating in Johnny's abduction. Noreen spoke with Bonacci and was struck by the details he shared about her son, which she believed Bonacci could only know if he had truly interacted with Johnny. While the FBI found Bonacci's story credible, they deemed it inconclusive, leaving Noreen with more questions than answers.

Decades have passed since Johnny's disappearance, and these questions have still not been answered. Not a single trace of evidence has surfaced, leaving Johnny's fate and whereabouts unknown.

MISSING
HAVE YOU SEEN THIS CHILD?
KYRON HORMAN
CONTACT: 55555555

THE COLD CASE OF KYRON HORMAN

PORTLAND, OREGON

2010

Kyron Horman was born on September 9, 2002, in Portland, Oregon. He lived with his father, Kaine Horman, and his stepmother, Terri Moulton, as well as the couple's baby daughter. At seven years old, Kyron was bright, energetic, and loved school, especially science. On the morning of June 4, 2010, Kyron was dropped off by his stepmother, Terri, for his school's science fair. Terri then left his school around 8:45 a.m., reportedly seeing Kyron walking down the hall toward his classroom; however, he never arrived for his first class and was marked absent.

That afternoon, Kaine and Terri walked to the bus stop together, expecting to pick up Kyron as usual. But when the bus arrived and Kyron wasn't on it, panic set in. The couple waited, but Kyron never came home from school, and no one had seen him since that morning. His parents reported him missing, but by then hours had passed since his last confirmed sighting. Police wasted no time launching an extensive search, and Kyron's disappearance quickly became one of Oregon's most high-profile missing persons cases.

Authorities initially focused on a two-mile radius around Skyline Elementary School but extended their efforts to Sauvie Island, located about six miles away. By June 12, just over a week after his disappearance, three hundred trained rescuers were on the ground, combing through dense wooded areas near the school. Over the course of ten days, more than 1,300 searchers participated in the effort. Despite their tireless work, not a single clue was found—no footprints, no personal belongings, nothing to indicate where Kyron had gone.

As the search pressed on, investigators began looking at those closest to Kyron, particularly his family. Kaine and Kyron's mother, Desiree Young, had divorced eight months into Desiree's pregnancy, when she was dealing with serious health issues. After having shared custody of Kyron, Kaine was granted full custody, during which time he married Terri Moulton. However, Kaine and Terri's marriage was far from perfect.

During investigations, authorities uncovered private emails that suggested Terri harbored resentment toward Kyron. In her emails, Terri blamed her marital problems on Kyron and expressed extreme frustration about her role in raising him. In addition to the emails, Terri failed two polygraph tests about the day Kyron disappeared and had major inconsistencies in her alibi. Her timeline for that morning placed her at two grocery stores until 10:10 a.m., but after that, her whereabouts became unclear. Added to the fact that she was the last known person to see Kyron, investigators began to shift their focus to Terri. Kaine and Desiree also began to publicly question Terri's role in the disappearance of their son.

Then police got their first lead when Terri's landscaper came forward and claimed that, six months before Kyron's disappearance, Terri had approached him with an offer to kill Kaine in exchange for money. Investigators immediately informed Kaine of the allegation, and his response was swift and decisive—he grabbed their nineteen-month-old daughter, left their home, and filed for both divorce and a restraining order against Terri. He believed that she may have hurt his son out of revenge. His suspicions were further fueled when two witnesses reported seeing an unidentified individual sitting inside Terri's truck outside Skyline Elementary on the morning Kyron vanished. Despite efforts to track this person down, they were never identified, and their potential involvement remained a mystery. Kyron's mother, Desiree, also became convinced that Terri was involved, stating, "I now believe, without a shadow of a doubt, that not only is she capable of hurting Kyron, but that it's clear she could have hurt him in the worst possible way."

In 2012, after years of frustration and unanswered questions, Desiree took legal action. She filed a civil lawsuit against Terri, alleging that she was responsible for kidnapping Kyron. However, in 2013, after realizing that legal action might interfere with the ongoing criminal investigation, Desiree made the difficult decision to drop the lawsuit.

With no physical evidence, eyewitness testimony, or forensic links to tie Terri to Kyron's disappearance, law enforcement eventually shifted their focus to other possible leads. However, none were ever identified. Terri eventually faded from the police's immediate radar, but she never stopped being a person of interest to Kyron's parents. To this day, they remain convinced that she knows far more than she has ever let on.

In 2016, after years of public suspicion and unanswered questions, Terri appeared on *Dr. Phil*. It was one of the only times she had spoken publicly about Kyron's disappearance, and she took the opportunity to deny any involvement. She insisted that she had no idea what happened to him and that she believed he had been kidnapped. During the interview, she introduced a new detail: She claimed that on the morning Kyron vanished, she had seen a man in a white pickup truck parked near Skyline Elementary School. According to her, the man was behaving strangely, pacing back and forth outside a nearby 7-Eleven for nearly an hour. Terri suggested that this man could have been responsible for Kyron's abduction. However, when pressed for more information, she had no further details to provide, and law enforcement was never able to identify or link anyone matching her description to the case.

Despite this claim, Terri remained the only person under intense scrutiny, though she was never officially charged with anything related to Kyron's disappearance. As the years have passed, hope for finding Kyron has dwindled, but his family has never stopped searching. His mother, Desiree, continues to fight for justice. Unfortunately, the case remains at a standstill. Law enforcement still receives occasional tips, but nothing substantial has ever come from them.

THE BARN

HUTKÓW, POLAND

2018

Mateusz Kawecki was a thirty-year-old man from the small village of Hutków, Poland, who worked in construction in Hanover, Germany. He lived in Hanover with his father, who also worked there, while his pregnant fiancée lived in the Polish village of Lipia Góra. Despite the distance, they maintained a strong relationship. So, when his fiancée was nearing her due date, Mateusz was eager to be there for the birth of their child.

On the night of March 28, 2018, Mateusz set off for Poland in his 1998 BMW—his fiancée eagerly anticipating his arrival the next morning. But Mateusz never arrived. Concerned, his father called him around 10:30 a.m., and Mateusz explained that he was stuck in terrible traffic in Szczecin, a town near the Germany–Poland border. At that point, he had roughly 133 miles left to Lipia Góra. Around the same time, he sent his fiancée a text message, reassuring her that he would be there in about two hours. But as the hours passed, everyone started to worry.

Mateusz's fiancée called him repeatedly, but each call went unanswered. Around 5:00 p.m., she contacted his sister, Katarzyna, who also lived in Hanover, hoping she had some information—but there was no response. With Mateusz still missing by nightfall, his mother went to the police to file a missing person report. However, authorities dismissed her concerns, stating it was too soon to report him missing. They assured her he would likely turn up soon.

By early April, with no sign of Mateusz, his family officially reported him missing in both Poland and Germany. Desperate for answers, they urged Polish authorities to track his phone, which remained active for at least a couple of days after his disappearance. However, because Mateusz used a German SIM card, the Polish police had no jurisdiction over it. The German authorities, on the other hand, claimed they couldn't help, as Mateusz had vanished in Poland. Investigators eventually checked CCTV footage at the Polish–German border, which showed no sign of his BMW entering Poland, raising more questions than answers. As time passed and authorities offered little assistance, the family realized they would have to take matters into their own hands.

Determined to find him, Mateusz's family retraced his entire route, scouring side roads and backstreets, stopping at small gas stations and stores, questioning staff or anyone who may have seen him pass through. They pleaded for access to security footage, put up missing person posters, and made emotional appearances on television in both Poland and Germany, publicly criticizing the police for failing to take his disappearance seriously. Despite their relentless efforts, months passed without any leads.

Then, on September 12, 2018, a neighbor stopped by Mateusz's mother's house in Hutków to talk about a growing concern. Since July, a terrible odor had been emanating from the Kaweckis' barn. The neighbors assumed it was the scent of a dead animal rotting in the summer heat, but as the stench grew worse, he asked permission to check it out. Mateusz's mother agreed.

The neighbor thoroughly searched the barn, and then he reached a space that was partially walled off, creating a separate, enclosed room with an attic space above. He climbed into the attic and immediately spotted a pile of clothing. As he stepped closer, he realized it wasn't just a pile of clothes, it was a severely decomposed body, including a severed head and a torso. After nearly six months it appeared that Mateusz had finally been found.

Investigators arrived at the barn to do a thorough search and uncovered even more unsettling clues. They found two rope nooses hanging from the roof, as well as some of Mateusz's teeth—presumably knocked out—stuck to his bloodstained clothes.

They found Mateusz's backpack, cell phone, and wallet, but his car keys and other personal belongings were still missing.

A formal investigation was launched, and forensic testing soon confirmed what Mateusz's family already feared—the remains were indeed his. His personal belongings, including the backpack and clothing, were examined for traces of additional DNA. Strangely, no foreign DNA was found anywhere in the barn. The police declared Mateusz's death a suicide and closed their investigation.

This ruling stunned Mateusz's family. To them, the brutal nature of the scene highly suggested foul play. They found it hard to believe that Mateusz could knock out his own teeth and sever his own head. Mateusz's family had also used the barn multiple times during the summer of 2018. They would have noticed a hanging body or smelled the unmistakable stench of decomposition. That said, the police stood by their conclusion—although they never released how the evidence led them to it.

Four days after Mateusz's remains were found, his family made yet another horrifying discovery—one that furthered their doubts that Mateusz took his own life. In a corner of the barn, they found one of Mateusz's shoes, with his amputated foot still inside it. This gruesome finding enraged his family, who knew that authorities didn't properly search the crime scene, yet they confidently declared Mateusz's death a suicide.

While the police refused to dig deeper, prosecutors took a different approach, conducting a more thorough investigation. They managed to gather significant evidence, including DNA analysis and phone records, that painted a different picture of Mateusz's final days. One of their more shocking revelations—Mateusz had lied to his family on the day he disappeared.

When he spoke to his father on March 29th, claiming to be stuck in traffic near Szczecin, close to the Germany–Poland border, he wasn't anywhere near there. In fact, receipts found among his belongings showed that he was still in Germany that morning. Investigators traced his movements and discovered he had taken a train to

Frankfurt, further contradicting his claim that he was driving to Lipia Góra. Then, nearly twenty-four hours after telling his loved ones he was already in Poland, he walked across the bridge to Słubice, a small Polish town on the border.

From there, his trail became even murkier. Mateusz appeared to check into a hotel with an unknown person, making it impossible to figure out their connection. His phone data placed him in Słubice for some time, but these new discoveries still left one question unanswered: How had Mateusz ended up dead, mutilated, and hidden in his family's barn—nearly three hundred miles away?

Despite extensive searches across both Poland and Germany, authorities have never been able to locate Mateusz's 1998 BMW.

Mateusz's case leaves behind more questions than answers. Many—including his own family—still firmly believe that he was murdered. The truth of what really happened to Mateusz Kawecki may forever remain a mystery.

THE CAVE DIVER

VORTEX SPRING, FLORIDA

2010

Ben McDaniel was the oldest of three sons born to Shelby and Patty McDaniel. He grew up in Collierville, Tennessee, and from a very young age had a relentless thirst for adventure. He went rock climbing with his youngest brother, Paul, but his favorite hobby was scuba diving, which he was involved in since he was fifteen. He found solace in the depths of the water, pushing himself to explore the unseen.

In the late 2000s, Ben's life started to spiral. His brother, Paul, suddenly passed away from what was believed to be a stroke but was later revealed to be an overdose. The pain of losing his brother was compounded by his divorce and by the failure of his construction business, which left him in severe debt. Ben owed nearly $50,000 to the IRS, a burden that weighed heavily on him.

Seeing how much their son was struggling, his parents encouraged him to move to Florida, offering him their vacation home as a place to regain control of his life. In 2010, he accepted their offer, hoping for a fresh start. His parents' house was located near Vortex Spring, a popular Florida diving spot known for its crystal-clear waters and complex cave systems. As an experienced and passionate diver, Ben visited the springs often and quickly became a regular, forming close relationships with fellow divers and other locals. It seemed like he was starting to move forward.

On August 18, 2010, Ben spent hours at Vortex Spring, completing his initial dive around midday. But when he resurfaced, there was something about his behavior that stood out to those who saw him—he seemed preoccupied, almost as if he were planning something. Witnesses recalled watching him carefully observe the entrance to one of the caves, scanning the area intently. Then he refilled his tanks, adjusted his equipment, and wrote in his dive log.

At around 7:30 p.m., Ben reentered the water. Ben regularly took evening dives, but the section of the cave he intended to enter was fifty-eight feet below the surface of Vortex Spring and off-limits, enclosed by a locked gate. The gate was meant to prevent untrained divers—Ben lacked his cave certification—from venturing into its dangerous depths. An employee, Eduardo Taran, was returning from a dive when he saw Ben near the gate. Instead of stopping him, Eduardo unlocked the gate, allowing Ben inside.

Eduardo was on duty with Chuck Cronin that night—both divers were familiar with Ben and regularly kept an eye out for him. They knew Ben to be a skilled diver and trusted his abilities, so they left to grab some coffee at Eduardo's house.

After Ben entered the water that night, his car stood undisturbed in the parking lot for two full days. Eduardo and Chuck claimed to have been too busy to notice, but once they did, they immediately called the authorities. When Ben's car was finally searched, they found his wallet containing a substantial amount of cash, his cell phone, his dive logs, and his keys. Later, when searching his home, they found his dog, Spooner, suffering from hunger after being left alone since Ben's dive. Worry that Ben had never resurfaced from his last dive started to set in, leaving his family and friends desperately clinging to hope.

Skilled divers immediately launched a rescue mission, descending into the dark, labyrinthine cave system in hopes of finding Ben or at least uncovering clues to what had happened. But no sign of him was found. The only things discovered were two oxygen tanks near the mouth of the cave, a detail that only deepened the mystery and fueled more urgent, extensive searches. Cadaver dogs searched the woods surrounding Vortex Spring but found nothing. Helicopters searched the nearby swamps, but still nothing.

As days passed with no progress, renowned cave rescue expert and technical cave diver Edd Sorenson was called in. Sorenson was known for diving deep into the treacherous passages, navigating areas few had ever reached. If Ben's body was trapped somewhere inside, Sorenson was confident he would find him. But after combing every accessible part of the cave, Sorenson concluded there was no sign of Ben inside the cave. Dead or alive, he simply wasn't there.

This revelation shattered previous assumptions and opened the floodgates to wild speculation. Some theorized that Ben had, in fact, died inside the cave, but that his body had somehow been lost through the spring's powerful underground currents, possibly lodged in an unsearchable crevice or swept out to sea. Others believed a more sinister fate had befallen him—that he was murdered, his body removed from the site before anyone noticed. And then, of course, there's the most controversial theory of all: Ben faked his own death. Given his financial struggles, recent divorce, and personal hardships, some speculate that he may have used his diving expertise to stage his disappearance and start a new life under a different identity. While there's no concrete evidence to support this, it remains one of the most debated possibilities in the case.

Suspecting foul play, Ben's family refused to sit back and wait for answers. They hired private investigator Lynn-Marie Carty in hopes that she could uncover the truth. Carty worked tirelessly, chasing down leads, conducting interviews, and scouring records for any trace of Ben. But despite her determination, her investigation only led to more frustration—there were no witnesses, no security footage, and no concrete evidence pointing to what had happened that night. However, Carty believed this was a homicide and that Ben's body was removed before authorities were contacted, and that the narrative of his disappearance was fabricated as a cover story.

Then, in 2013, after years of unanswered questions and no sign of Ben, the state of Florida officially issued his death certificate, without any substantial proof that he had died. It was a devastating moment for his family, who never got to say goodbye or any real closure. Despite the state's ruling, Ben's family refused to give up. To them, the absence of a body meant the possibility that he was still out there, somewhere, alive.

To this day, no trace of Ben McDaniel has ever been found. No body, no diving equipment, no definitive evidence. The theories surrounding his fate have only grown more complex with time, and the truth remains just as elusive as it was the night he disappeared.

A HUSBAND'S SECRET

WEST VALLEY CITY, UTAH
2009

Susan Powell was a bright, loving person—warm, kindhearted, and adored by her family and friends. Susan was a devout member of the Church of Jesus Christ of Latter-day Saints in Puyallup, Washington, where she grew up. At one of the church's functions, she met Josh Powell, who proposed within days of meeting her. She was nineteen years old when they married at the Portland Oregon Temple on April 6, 2001.

After their wedding, the couple moved in with Josh's father, Steven Powell, who was not only controlling over Josh but eventually displayed an obsessive infatuation with Susan—stealing her underwear, recording her in secret, reading her journal, and even openly admitting his feelings for her. Growing increasingly uneasy, Susan and Josh left Washington and moved to Utah.

In Utah, Susan focused on her budding career as a broker while Josh struggled to hold down a job, leaving them with growing financial stress. Despite their struggles, Susan and Josh welcomed two sons into their lives, Charles and Braden Powell. With the addition of two young children, Susan and Josh's relationship started to unravel. Josh refused to attend church with his family, spent their money recklessly, exhibited controlling behavior, and dismissed Susan's continued concerns about his father's disturbing behavior, often siding with Steven whenever Susan raised concerns about his obsession.

By 2007, Josh had driven the family into financial ruin, accumulating over $200,000 in debt before finally declaring bankruptcy. Realizing the severity of her situation, Susan began documenting her fears. In June 2008, she secretly wrote a will, expressing her growing distress, including the statement "If I die, it may not be an accident, even if it looks like one." She also detailed how Josh had threatened to leave the country and sue her if she ever tried to divorce him. A month later, she even filmed evidence of the property damage that she said Josh had caused in their home.

On December 6, 2009, Susan and her two sons attended church, just like any other Sunday. After church, a neighbor stopped by their home—the last person outside the family to ever see Susan alive. The next morning, when Charles and Braden never showed up at daycare, the staff attempted to contact both Susan and Josh, but neither answered their phones. Growing concerned, the staff reached out to Josh's mother, who, sensing something was terribly wrong, called the police.

Detective Ellis Maxwell arrived at the Powell home on the morning of December 7. As he stepped inside, he found all of Susan's belongings still there—her purse, her keys, everything she would have needed. There were no signs of forced entry or an obvious struggle, and nothing to suggest she had run away. But then he noticed something strange—two large fans blowing directly onto a damp spot on the carpet, as if someone was desperately trying to dry or remove something.

It wasn't until 5 p.m. that evening—hours after police had already been looking for the family—that Josh returned home with his sons. When police questioned him, he said that he had taken his boys on a spontaneous camping trip.

The detectives found his explanation suspicious for several reasons: His sons were two and four years old, it was a weeknight, and it was freezing cold outside. As the officers pressed Josh for details, they noticed his answers were becoming increasingly bizarre. After talking, the police searched Josh's car and found Susan's phone, as well as several tools. When asked about both her phone and the tools, Josh had no explanation. While police had no real evidence or reason to press charges, they did seize his car to be processed for evidence.

The following day, Josh rented a car and drove it eight hundred miles, before returning it to the Salt Lake City airport just twenty-four hours later. He didn't share with anyone where he was going or why, and the police never got a clear answer from him, either.

By December 9, police executed a formal search of the Powell home, uncovering evidence that suggested something terrible had happened to Susan. They found traces of her blood on the floor, a life insurance policy taken out in her name, and a handwritten note from Susan herself, expressing fear for her life.

Next, they learned that days after the alleged camping trip, Charles told his teacher that his mother had gone with them but was now dead. At daycare, Braden had drawn a disturbing picture of three people in a van and told one of the caregivers, "Mommy was in the trunk." Around the same time, police also discovered that Josh had liquidated Susan's IRA shortly after her disappearance, further fueling speculation about his involvement. But without Susan's body, they still couldn't arrest Josh.

After Susan vanished, Josh and his two boys moved back to Puyallup to live with Josh's father, Steven. During the investigation, Steven became a person of interest when police learned about his obsession with Susan. They eventually got a warrant to search his house where they found nearly 4,500 photos of Susan—taken without her knowledge—and child sex abuse materials. Steven was eventually charged with voyeurism and possession of child pornography.

Josh's brother Michael Powell was yet another family member who police suspected was involved in Susan's disappearance. They started questioning him after they discovered his abandoned Ford Taurus at a wrecking yard in Oregon. The location and disposal of the vehicle immediately raised red flags. When detectives questioned him about it, Michael was evasive, offering no clear explanation.

Josh eventually lost custody of his two sons to Susan's parents and was ordered to undergo a psychological evaluation. He was, however, granted visitations with his sons several times a week, supervised by a social worker. On February 5, his social worker, Elizabeth Griffin Hall, arrived at Josh's home at 12:30 p.m. with Charles and Braden. As soon as the boys stepped through the front door, Josh slammed it shut, locking Elizabeth outside. Josh then attacked his sons with an axe, inflicting brutal injuries to their necks and heads. He then doused the house and his sons in gasoline and set it ablaze. Moments later, the house exploded in a fiery inferno, killing Josh, Charles, and Braden.

Perhaps Josh realized that the walls were closing in on him. With law enforcement scrutinizing his every move and his custody of Charles and Braden slipping away, he may have felt he had no way out. Rather than face the consequences of his actions, he chose the most horrific path imaginable: murdering his own sons before taking his own life. About one year later, his brother Michael also took his own life by jumping from the top of a building to his death.

To this day, Susan Powell has never been found. There remain no clear answers for those who love her, and perhaps no way to fully piece together what happened to her that fateful night in December 2009.

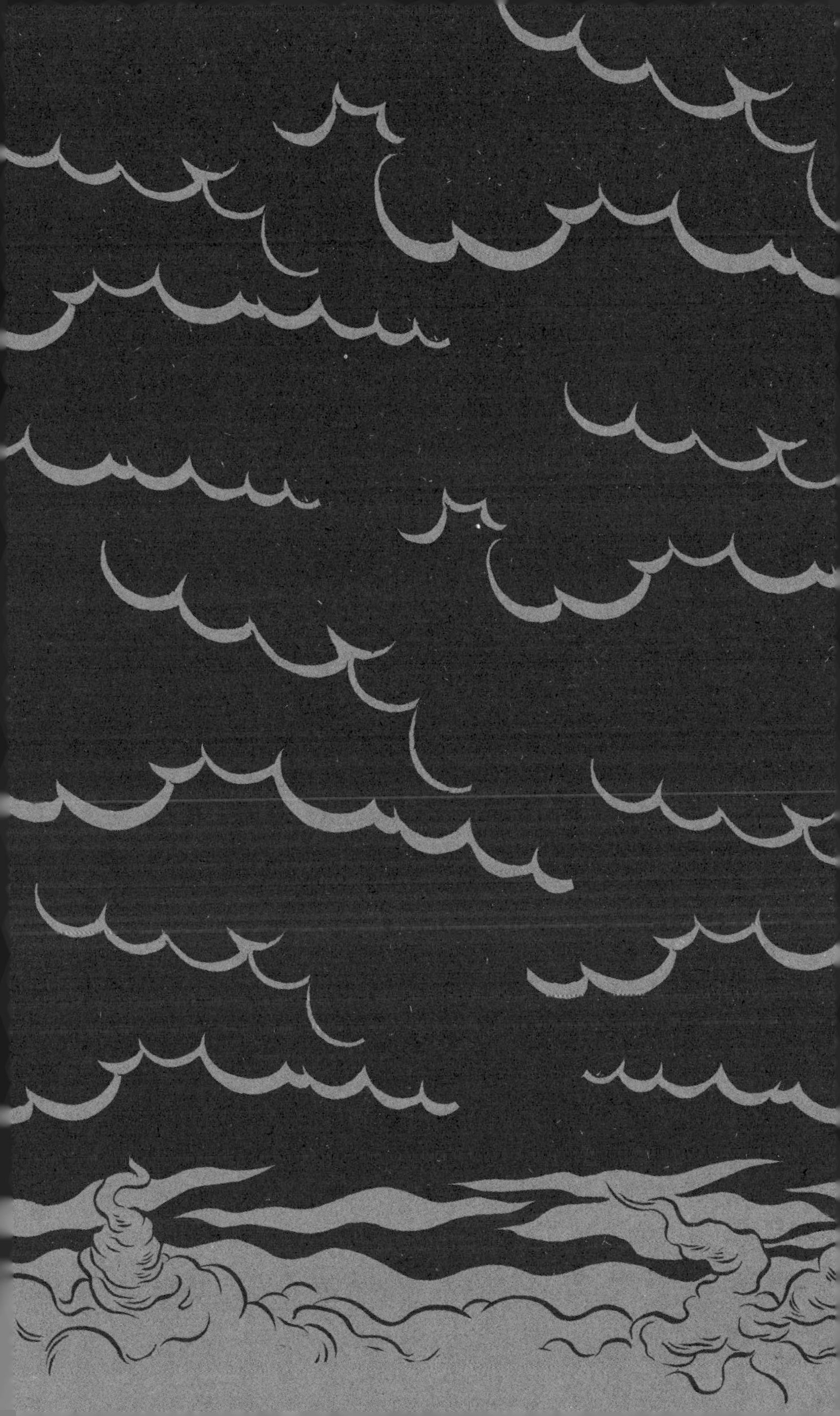

CHAPTER THREE

THE INVADERS

Alien Encounters, UFOs, and Other Extraterrestrial Mysteries

THE FIRST ABDUCTION

WHITE MOUNTAINS, NEW HAMPSHIRE 1961

Their account would go on to become one of the most famous and highly scrutinized alien abduction cases in history. While some believed their story, others dismissed it as a fabrication or a trick of the mind. But whether fact or fiction, the case of Betty and Barney Hill remains one of the most compelling and mysterious UFO encounters ever recorded.

Betty and Barney Hill were an ordinary couple from New Hampshire. Betty was a social worker specializing in child welfare cases and Barney was a postal worker. They both typically worked long hours, and in addition, they often volunteered their free time. As an interracial couple in the 1960s, the couple was deeply committed to advancing the Civil Rights Movement. They were both members of the NAACP and very involved with helping at their local church. After agreeing to take a much-needed break, they set off on a relaxing getaway from Montreal to Niagara Falls.

After three days of vacationing, on the night of September 19, 1961, the couple began their long journey home. It was around 10:00 p.m. when they noticed a bright light in the sky. At first, Barney dismissed it as an airplane or perhaps a satellite, but Betty was uneasy. The light didn't behave like any aircraft she had ever seen before. It moved erratically—zigzagging, shifting speeds, and making no noise. As they drove along the dark, desolate highway, an unsettling realization crept in: The light seemed to be following them.

Curious, they pulled over to walk their dog and get a better look. Betty took binoculars with her while Barney, always mindful of safety, retrieved his pistol in case of any large animals in the area. As they observed the strange object, they tried to rationalize what they were seeing. Convinced it must be a conventional aircraft, they got back into the car and resumed their drive—but Betty's unease remained.

Her anxiety was fueled by a recent conversation with her sister, who had told her a story about a UFO encounter. Betty couldn't shake the feeling that they were experiencing something beyond explanation. The object continued to follow them, hovering at a distance before drawing close, only to retreat again.

Suddenly, the UFO accelerated at an astonishing speed, closing the distance between itself and the Hills' car. It descended directly in front of them, hovering just twenty feet above the ground. As they realized there was no clear escape, a sense of pure dread washed over them.

Barney, overwhelmed with both fear and curiosity, told Betty to stay in the car. Grabbing his pistol and binoculars, he sprinted toward the strange craft for a closer look. As he focused in on the craft, his blood ran cold. Through a large window on the ship, he saw a group of humanlike beings staring back at him. Their piercing, unnatural gaze sent a wave of panic through him. Overcome with terror, Barney turned and ran back to the car, shouting frantically, "The beings are going to capture us!"

They wasted no time—Betty and Barney sped off, desperate to escape. But their nightmare had only just begun. A strange noise, similar to a microwave's hum, filled the car, growing louder and more intense. Suddenly, the vehicle began to vibrate violently, the controls unresponsive. Then darkness.

The next thing they knew, two hours had passed. They found themselves thirty-five miles away from the last place they remembered, with no recollection of how they got there. Their dog was under the passenger seat, trembling. A deep sense of unease settled over them. Once they arrived home, Barney discovered that his binocular strap had been torn, but he didn't recall any struggle. Betty's dress was ripped and covered in a strange pink powder. Their watches had stopped working entirely, frozen in time. Their car had mysterious, perfectly circular marks on its surface.

Desperate for answers, the Hills contacted a nearby Air Force base, reporting their encounter in the hopes of an explanation—but nothing came of it. As days passed, the weight of the experience began to take a psychological toll on them. Both developed severe anxiety, plagued by disturbing dreams, unexplained ulcers, and relentless insomnia. Barney, however, suffered one particularly strange symptom, a bizarre cluster of warts forming around his groin. The couple knew, deep down, that something had been done to them.

Betty's dreams began to consume her, bleeding into her daily life with an intensity she couldn't ignore. Desperate for answers, on December 14, 1963, she and Barney sought out Dr. Benjamin Simon, a psychiatrist specializing in hypnotherapy. Under hypnosis, the missing hours from that night came flooding back. Betty and Barney recounted being escorted up a large ramp into the spacecraft, surrounded by the same small, gray-skinned beings Barney had seen through the ship's window. Once inside, the aliens informed them, "We're going to run some basic tests."

The tests were far from ordinary. The beings examined their eyes, ears, and nose, meticulously documenting their findings. They collected samples of their skin and hair, studying their anatomy in ways no human doctor ever had. Betty remembered the aliens performing a pregnancy test on her by inserting a long, terrifyingly large needle into her abdomen. The pain was sharp and immediate, making it one of the most traumatic parts of the entire ordeal.

Barney's memories were equally unsettling. He recalled being forcefully grabbed, which he believed caused his binoculars to break. Along with the standard tests, the beings also took a semen sample from him, though he couldn't explain how. Both Betty and Barney described the aliens as short, gray-skinned creatures with oversize heads and large, dark eyes.

One of the most compelling aspects of their account, the detail that has convinced many believers, was Betty's description of a star system she claimed the aliens showed her while aboard the craft. Under hypnosis, she recalled seeing a three-dimensional star map, which she later re-created from memory. At the time, the arrangement of stars didn't seem to match any known system, and skeptics dismissed it as a product of her imagination. However, years later, astronomers found that her map bore a striking resemblance to the Zeta Reticuli star system, a binary star system located about thirty-nine light-years away from Earth. The accuracy of her depiction left many people questioning how she could have possibly known about it, given that the system had not been widely studied or mapped in detail at the time.

Despite the extraordinary details that emerged under hypnosis, not everyone believed their story. Dr. Simon himself remained skeptical. He theorized that Betty's persistent nightmares had influenced Barney's recollection, creating a shared false memory rooted in deep-seated stress and anxiety. Certain details of their experience even changed over time—notably, their original description of the aliens evolved.

Both Betty and Barney passed away years ago, but even on their deathbeds, they never wavered. They stood by their story until the very end, insisting that what they experienced that night was real. Despite criticism from skeptics and experts who dismissed their memories as hallucinations, dreams, or false recollections influenced by external factors, the Hills never once retracted their claims. Betty spent the rest of her life studying UFO phenomena, convinced that what had happened to her and Barney was part of something much bigger than anyone realized.

Betty and Barney's account would go on to become one of the most famous and highly scrutinized alien abduction cases in history. Some UFO researchers consider it the Rosetta Stone of alien abduction stories, a case that set the precedent for thousands of similar reports.

THE PASCAGOULA ALIEN ABDUCTION

PASCAGOULA, MISSISSIPPI

1973

On the evening of October 11, 1973, nineteen-year-old Calvin Parker and forty-two-year-old Charles Hickson were fishing near an old shipyard along the Pascagoula River in Mississippi. The night was calm, and they were excited that Charles had just caught a fish. But their celebration was cut short when an odd zipping sound echoed behind them. The noise was unlike anything they had ever heard—an eerie, mechanical hum that sent a chill through the air. A sudden glow of blue lights reflected off the water, catching their attention. At first, they assumed law enforcement was approaching to ask them to leave, but when they turned around to investigate, they reportedly saw something massive—a thirty-foot-long, football-shaped craft hovering just above the ground. It had two portholes on its smooth metallic surface, and before they could react, a door snapped open. A bright white light burst out from within, momentarily blinding them. Then three figures emerged from the craft.

The beings were around five feet tall, but their appearance was unlike anything Calvin and Charles had ever seen. Their skin was a wrinkled, grayish color, and they moved in an unnatural, floating motion. Their elongated arms ended in clawlike hands, almost resembling crabs or insects. Their heads seemed to merge directly with their shoulders, lacking a visible neck, and where their ears should have been, they had long, pointed protrusions—almost identical to their noses, which extended about two inches straight out from their faces. They had large, elephant-like feet.

Overcome with terror, Calvin fainted on the spot. Charles, frozen with fear, could only watch in horror as two of the creatures seized him. A strange numbing sensation spread through his body, making him unable to resist. The third being grabbed Calvin, who remained unconscious, and without hesitation, the strange entities floated back toward their craft, carrying the two men with them.

Once inside the strange craft, Calvin and Charles found themselves completely at the mercy of their captors. There were no chairs, no visible control panels, and no recognizable technology—just a sterile, white room with rounded walls that felt otherworldly. Instead of walking, the two men were moved effortlessly through the air, as if they were floating. They felt no pain, no resistance—just a strange numbness.

At one point, they were separated and taken to different rooms. Charles later recalled that a machine resembling a giant red eye hovered over him, scanning his body. The five-foot-tall beings stood around him, their clawed hands never touching him, yet somehow he felt as though they were studying every inch of him. Calvin's experience was similar, though he struggled to recall the details—his mind clouded by fear and confusion. Then, just as suddenly as it began, the ordeal was over. The next thing they knew, they were back on the riverbank, standing exactly where they had been before. The craft hovered silently for a moment before taking off into the night sky and disappearing without a trace. As it vanished, Charles heard a voice inside his head—a telepathic message from the beings themselves: "We are peaceful. We meant you no harm."

Shaken and terrified, the two men drove straight to the Jackson County Sheriff's Office and reported the entire incident to Sheriff Fred Diamond and Captain Glenn Ryder. They described the creatures' appearance, the strange floating sensation, the experiments, and the giant red eye in vivid detail. However, neither of them could remember if the beings had eyes or what the inside of the spacecraft looked like beyond its rounded walls. For Charles, what stuck out the most wasn't the aliens or the ship—it was the sheer terror on Calvin's face. He had never seen a man so afraid. Coming from Charles, a Korean War veteran who had witnessed the horrors of combat, that statement carried a lot of weight.

As expected, Captain Ryder didn't believe them. But instead of dismissing them outright, he decided to set a trap. He and the sheriff stepped out of the interrogation room, secretly leaving a tape recorder running—in the hope of catching the two men slipping up and proving their story was an elaborate hoax. But what they heard shook them to their core. Charles's voice trembled as he muttered, "I thought I'd been through enough of Hell on this earth, and now I've got to go through something like this." Calvin, still in shock, whispered, "But they could have...you know...I guess they...Well, they could have harmed us. They had us. They could have done anything to us. I just want to cry right now. What's so damn bad about it is nobody's going to believe us." The two men were genuinely terrified. They weren't putting on a show for the sheriff. They were having a real emotional breakdown. Captain Ryder started to believe them.

Further investigation uncovered that several other police officers in the area had also reported seeing strange UFOs around the same time as Calvin and Charles's alleged abduction. This revelation added an unexpected layer of credibility to their claims, and soon, the Pascagoula abduction story spread like wildfire, captivating both believers and skeptics alike. Eventually, the two men underwent hypnosis and multiple lie detector tests in an effort to uncover more details about their experience—but no evidence of deception was ever found, leaving many wondering if they had truly encountered something beyond human understanding. However, with no physical evidence to support their claims, the mystery of their abduction remained unsolved.

In 1983, Charles took matters into his own hands, writing and publishing a book detailing their harrowing experience. It was titled *UFO Contact at Pascagoula*. Calvin, however, chose a different path—for years, he largely avoided the spotlight, staying silent about the incident. In 1993, Calvin founded UFO Investigators, a company dedicated to sharing stories about UFO encounters. Though he occasionally attended UFO conventions, he still preferred to keep a low profile regarding his experience.

That was until Charles passed away from a heart attack at the age of eighty. His passing deeply affected Calvin, reigniting his desire to share his side of the story with the world.

In 2018, Calvin also published a book titled *Pascagoula: The Closest Encounter, My Story*. His book sparked a wave of new testimonies—countless individuals came forward, claiming they had also seen a UFO that very night. Many of these witnesses were credible sources, further reinforcing the notion that something truly extraordinary had occurred. For Calvin, this was a powerful validation—he and Charles were no longer the only ones who saw something unexplainable that night.

Sadly, in August 2023, Calvin Parker passed away after a battle with kidney cancer. But like Charles, he never once wavered in his account of what happened on that fateful night in 1973. Despite decades of debate, skepticism, and investigation, the Pascagoula abduction remains one of the most compelling and mysterious UFO encounters in history. Whether one chooses to believe it or not, one thing is undeniable—Calvin Parker and Charles Hickson went to their graves standing by their story.

THE DAY THEY CAME

RUWA, ZIMBABWE
1994

On September 16, 1994, approximately 250 children were playing outside during their usual midmorning break, around 10:00 a.m., at Ariel School, a private elementary school in Zimbabwe. Then something unusual caught the attention of sixty-two students. Three silver orbs appeared in the sky above the school, moving in an erratic manner. The objects would vanish in a flash of bright light, only to reappear in a different location seconds later. This happened three times in a row, until, to the children's shock, one of the objects descended toward the school and landed in an open field just beyond the playground.

Then the students reported seeing small humanoid figures emerge from the craft. The beings had waxy, almost translucent skin, oversize heads, and large, black, penetrating eyes that seemed to stare right through them. According to the children, the beings did not speak but instead conveyed messages telepathically, warning them about the future of Earth's environment. The message was clear: Humanity needed to protect the planet before it was too late.

The strange encounter was over in the matter of fifteen minutes, yet it still left many of the children terrified, causing some to break down in tears. As soon as the beings vanished, the children rushed back inside, frantically telling their teachers what had just happened. However, their accounts were quickly dismissed as overactive imaginations.

But the story didn't end there. Later that evening, many of the students told their parents about the bizarre encounter. The next morning, a group of concerned parents arrived at the school, eager to discuss what their children had seen. Word of the strange sighting quickly spread, eventually catching the attention of renowned UFO investigator Cynthia Hind, who had been actively tracking UFO activity in South Africa. But when she heard about what had transpired at Ariel School, she knew this case was different—and it could be one of the most significant UFO encounters ever recorded.

Cynthia Hind wasted no time. She immediately visited Ariel School to personally interview the children about what they had witnessed. To ensure accuracy, she spoke to them in small groups of two to six, allowing them to recount their experiences in detail. As they described what they had seen, the children were also asked to draw the UFO and the beings they encountered.

Their descriptions were unusually consistent. Many of the children claimed to have seen a small figure dressed in a black, shiny bodysuit. The being had long black hair that reached its shoulders, and its large, penetrating eyes sat lower on the face than those of a human. One student, Barry D., witnessed three unidentified objects flying over the school, each with flashing red lights. He described how a small humanoid emerged from one of the crafts, and when it realized the children were watching, it vanished—only for a similar figure to reappear a short distance away moments later.

Cynthia also collected between thirty and forty drawings from the students, depicting the strange visitors and their craft. Some sketches were vague, while others were highly detailed, but the most astonishing part was that almost all of them resembled a classic flying saucer. Cynthia believed they were telling the truth. Cynthia then reached out to Dr. John Mack, a Harvard psychiatrist and Pulitzer Prize–winning researcher, to assist in her investigation. Dr. Mack had extensively studied alien abduction cases and was well-versed in paranormal psychology, making him the perfect expert to analyze the children's testimonies.

During Dr. Mack's interviews, the children opened up even more than before. Many reiterated that the aliens communicated with them telepathically, delivering an urgent message about the state of the planet. One fifth-grade student, Francis, recalled that the alien had warned him, "Pollution mustn't be." Another student, Emma, shared a similar account, stating, "I think they want people to know that we're actually making harm on this world, and we mustn't get too technological." The more Dr. Mack listened, the more he became convinced that these children were not fabricating their experiences.

There are many skeptics of the Ariel School encounter, each with their own theories or explanations. Some argue that the event was simply a case of mass hysteria, where childhood imagination, group psychology, and external influences combined to create a shared illusion. Others suggest that while the students may have witnessed something unusual, it does not necessarily mean that it was extraterrestrial in nature—perhaps it was a misinterpretation of a natural or man-made phenomenon.

One of the biggest counterarguments revolves around an event that occurred just days before the alleged encounter: Strange lights had been seen in the sky across southern Africa, prompting numerous reports of UFO activity. Even Cynthia Hind herself witnessed these lights. But investigations later revealed that what many believed to be an extraterrestrial spectacle was actually the reentry of the Zenit-2 rocket, which had launched the Cosmos 2290 satellite. This space debris had burned up in the atmosphere, creating a brilliant display that could have fueled the children's imagination.

Another key argument challenges Cynthia's claim that the children had no prior exposure to UFO lore or alien imagery. While Ariel School was in a rural part of Zimbabwe, it was not completely isolated. The school was near Harare, the capital city, and many of the students had access to television, books, and international media. By the 1990s, aliens and UFOs were already deeply embedded in popular culture, thanks to movies like *E.T. the Extra-Terrestrial* (1982) and *The X-Files* (1993), which had gained worldwide recognition. Skeptics argue that the children's descriptions of large-eyed, humanoid beings could have been influenced by existing depictions of extraterrestrials in media, rather than a real encounter.

To their dying day, Dr. John Mack and Cynthia Hind—two respected researchers in the field—stood by their conclusion that the children had not fabricated their story. Mack was so convinced of their sincerity that he risked his reputation at Harvard to defend their claims. The children—now adults—also remain steadfast, with many still emotionally affected by what they saw that day.

The Ariel School sighting remains one of the most compelling and well-documented UFO encounters in history. The case continues to raise intriguing questions that skeptics and believers alike struggle to answer—keeping the Ariel Phenomenon alive in UFO lore, even decades later.

THE PILOT WHO DISAPPEARED INTO THIN AIR

BASS STRAIT, AUSTRALIA

1978

On October 21, 1978, twenty-year-old pilot Frederick Valentich took off on what was supposed to be a routine training flight over the Bass Strait, the unpredictable body of water separating mainland Australia from Tasmania. He was piloting a Cessna 182L, a small and relatively lightweight aircraft, well-suited for his level of experience. While Frederick had logged around 150 hours of flight time, he was still considered an inexperienced pilot.

At 7:04 p.m., he made a disturbing transmission to Melbourne Flight Service, reporting that a mysterious aircraft was following him at an altitude of 4,500 feet. However, air traffic control assured him that no other planes were registered in his vicinity. Despite this, Frederick insisted that he could clearly see something in the sky with him. He described the craft as having four bright landing lights, which shone intensely against the evening sky. The aircraft, according to him, was moving at incredible speeds, far beyond what he had ever witnessed before.

Over the next few minutes, Frederick's concern escalated into fear. The unidentified aircraft wasn't just flying in a straight line—it was darting around him, appearing in different positions, and even orbiting above his plane. He speculated that the other pilot was deliberately toying with him, but the way it maneuvered was unlike anything he had encountered. Then the engine of Frederick's Cessna began to sputter, and he urgently radioed Melbourne Flight Service to report it. Controllers, now alarmed, asked him once more to identify the aircraft. "It isn't an aircraft," he replied.

Those were Frederick's final words before the transmission was abruptly cut off, replaced only by a seventeen-second metallic, scraping sound—and then complete silence. An immediate air and sea rescue mission was launched, scouring more than one thousand square miles of ocean and coastline, but they were unable to find any trace of Frederick or his plane. Authorities, including the Australian Department of Transport, continued to search tirelessly, hoping to find wreckage, debris, or any clue that could explain what happened to Frederick and his plane. But nothing was ever found—no crash site, no floating remains, not even a trace of the Cessna's location signal. After four days, his disappearance was presumed fatal, and the search was officially called off.

Five years after Frederick vanished, a small but significant discovery reignited interest in the case. An engine cowl flap—a component from an aircraft's engine—washed ashore on Flinders Island, located in the Bass Strait. Investigators examined the part and determined that it matched the same type of aircraft Frederick had been flying, and its serial number was within the same range as his Cessna 182L. Though it was only a single fragment, it was the first and only piece of evidence ever linked to his disappearance.

As speculation around the case grew, Guido Valentich, Frederick's father, revealed that his son had been a firm believer in UFOs and often spoke about his fear of being attacked or even abducted by extraterrestrial beings while flying. A few days before his disappearance, Frederick had also shared his fears of being abducted by aliens with his girlfriend. This revelation fueled the UFO community's belief that Frederick was not just missing but had been taken. Ufologists pointed to Frederick's radio transmissions—during which he described seeing strange green lights around the unidentified aircraft—as potential evidence of extraterrestrial involvement. That same evening, multiple eyewitnesses in the area also reported seeing green lights in the sky.

One notable claim came from a UFO research group called Ground Saucer Watch, based in Phoenix, Arizona. They stated that on the day of Frederick's disappearance, they had captured photographs allegedly showing a fast-moving object emerging from the water near Cape Otway Lighthouse—the very area where Frederick had last been seen on radar. However, these images were deemed too blurry and inconclusive to confirm anything.

Another UFO group alleged that a farmer, whose identity remains unknown, had witnessed a thirty-meter-long craft hovering over his farm, and that Frederick's missing aircraft was stuck to the side of the UFO, leaking oil. The farmer's account was never officially documented, and despite repeated attempts by UFO researchers to track him down, he was never found.

Decades later, the mystery of what happened to Frederick Valentich remains unsolved. The Australian government has put forth several possible explanations, but none have been confirmed due to the lack of definitive evidence. One theory suggests mechanical failure—that his Cessna 182L may have suffered an issue that led to a crash into the ocean. Another possibility is pilot disorientation, a condition where a pilot loses their sense of direction, especially while flying at night over open water. If Frederick had become disoriented, he could have unknowingly entered a dangerous spiral dive, leading to a fatal crash.

Some have proposed an even more unusual theory—that Frederick staged his own disappearance. They suggest that he may have faked the UFO encounter as a cover for his escape, either to start a new life elsewhere or to take his own life. His friends and family strongly refuted the idea that he would vanish on purpose, stating that it was completely out of character for him. By all accounts, Frederick was passionate about aviation and had no known financial, personal, or emotional struggles that would have driven him to such an extreme decision.

The disappearance of Frederick Valentich remains one of the most baffling and debated aviation mysteries of all time, often compared to the legendary case of Amelia Earhart. Unlike many other aviation incidents, where wreckage is eventually discovered or a plausible explanation emerges, this case offers no closure—only speculation. To this day, it is considered Australia's greatest unexplained disappearance, a case that has left scientists, investigators, and UFO enthusiasts alike grappling for answers. Every few years, new theories resurface, and yet none can definitively explain what happened that night over the Bass Strait.

A TOWN THAT CHANGED FOREVER

BERKSHIRE COUNTY, MASSACHUSETTS

1969

As the clock struck 8:00 p.m. on September 1, 1969, around forty residents across multiple towns in Berkshire County, Massachusetts, noticed unusual lights in the sky, unlike anything they had seen before. These weren't the standard blinking lights of airplanes or helicopters—they were brilliant, colorful orbs that darted erratically across the sky at impossible speeds, performing acrobatics that defied physics. Witnesses described seeing a large, disk-shaped craft hovering in the air, its movements too smooth and precise to be anything man-made.

Eventually, reports flooded in from all over the county—men, women, and children all claimed to have seen the same otherworldly phenomenon. Strangely, many of them experienced lost time, unable to recall exactly how long the event lasted. One specific account involved nine-year-old Thomas Reed and his family. Thomas, his mother, his grandmother, and his brother were driving through town when they noticed a massive disk-shaped object in the sky. It wasn't just floating—it was following them. The craft, reportedly larger than a football field, loomed over their car, casting an intense, blinding light that engulfed the entire vehicle. Suddenly, the family was pulled into the air, their car vanishing into the brightness.

According to Thomas, he was transported to what he could only describe as a hangar-like structure, a space so vast it felt as large as a field. He remembered seeing fluorescent tubelike lights, and a circular hallway with a Y-shaped configuration, seemingly designed to control movement. The environment was so advanced that even as a child, he knew it was something beyond human technology. Then, just as suddenly as it began, the experience was over. Thomas regained consciousness inside the family's car, now mysteriously parked a mile away from where they were abducted. His grandmother and mother had switched seats, yet no one could recall moving. The entire family was left shaken and disoriented, struggling to process what had just happened.

Melanie Kirchdorfer, another eyewitness, was spending the evening at Lake Mansfield in Great Barrington with her family. She recalled that when her father was backing into a parking spot, their car was suddenly engulfed in an intense, blinding light. The moment the light hit them, everyone in the car was panic-stricken. But instead of fleeing, Melanie's father got out of the car and chased the mysterious light, despite Melanie's desperate pleas for him to stop.

The next thing Melanie knew, she was levitating. Then, in an instant, she was no longer at the lake—she was on the ship. Though her memories of the event were fragmented, another witness, Tom Warner, later confirmed seeing Melanie on the craft with him—her face filled with absolute terror. However, Melanie had no recollection of Tom. Instead, she vividly remembered being inside a strange room alongside several other children. One by one, the children disappeared, vanishing without a trace, until she was the only one left. Then, in an instant, she woke up at the lake—alone, disoriented, confused, and terrified. With no sign of her family, she had no choice but to walk home, baffled by what had just happened.

The U.S. government was alerted to the Berkshire UFO encounter, but their stance on UFOs during this time was largely shaped by Project Blue Book—a U.S. Air Force program that scrutinized thousands of UFO sightings from 1952 to 1969. While many of Project Blue Book's investigations were dismissed as misidentified weather balloons or other known phenomena, a select few, including the

Berkshire UFO sighting, remain unsolved. Even after Project Blue Book was officially terminated, reports suggest that the government never actually stopped investigating UFO encounters. Instead, studies into unidentified aerial phenomena allegedly continued in secret, with classified research programs still running to this day. This has led many to consider if the Berkshire incident should be reexamined, given that new technologies and analysis might offer fresh insights.

Many skeptics have attempted to explain away the event as mass hysteria, overactive imaginations, or simple misidentification. However, according to Dr. Robert Powell, a respected scientist and investigator, the case is particularly notable because of the sheer number of credible witnesses—children and adults, strangers from all over—who described the same disk-shaped craft and bright lights, levitation experiences, and unexplained lapses in time.

Dr. David Jacobs, a renowned UFO researcher and professor at Temple University, has studied the Berkshire case extensively. He believes that this incident may not be an isolated event but rather part of a broader pattern of UFO sightings that challenge our current scientific understanding. According to Jacobs, cases like the Berkshire incident suggest that there is more to these encounters than simple mistaken identity—that there may be something genuinely unexplained happening beyond the limits of what we currently comprehend.

To this day, the Berkshire UFO encounter remains an unsolved mystery, one that has left permanent emotional scars on those who lived through it. Some witnesses refuse to discuss what happened, fearing ridicule or disbelief. Others, however, have spent their lives searching for answers, determined to prove that what they saw was real. The case continues to be a major topic of discussion among UFO researchers, historians, and enthusiasts from around the world.

THE LITTLE RED-EYED CREATURE

VARGINHA, BRAZIL

1996

On January 20, 1996, two sisters, Liliane and Valquíria Silva, along with their friend Kátia Andrade Xavier, were enjoying each other's company on a quiet afternoon near Jardim Andere in Varginha, Brazil, simply making their way home. As they walked across a vacant lot, hidden among the weeds and crouched low to the ground, they saw a creature unlike anything they had ever seen before. It stood about four feet tall, with massive, bloodred eyes that seemed to glow in the dim light. Its head was abnormally large and shaped like a V with three distinct bumps on top. Its brown skin appeared slick and oily, and it gave off a putrid stench—a sickly mix of sulfur and ammonia, like rotting eggs. The creature seemed frail and frightened, its large eyes reflecting both sadness and fear. For a moment, the girls locked eyes with the being, paralyzed by fear and confusion. Then panic set in. Terrified, they ran home, screaming that they had seen the devil.

The Silva girls' mother, shaken by their hysterical state, immediately called neighbors and friends, and the story spread like wildfire. Fear and curiosity gripped the town as more people began reporting sightings of the strange creature—and the crashed UFO it had seemingly come from. Just one week earlier, a local pilot named Carlos de Souza claimed to have seen a strange cigar-shaped craft—roughly the size of a school bus—flying low over Varginha. The craft appeared to be in distress, trailing thick white smoke as it struggled to maintain altitude. Believing it was in trouble, Carlos followed its trajectory and eventually found himself in an open field littered with strange metallic debris. The lightweight metal pieces had an unusual, almost foil-like texture—but when he bent them, they snapped right back into shape. He also described a foul, chemical smell that lingered in the air. Before Carlos could investigate further, military personnel in unmarked vehicles swarmed the site. They ordered him to leave immediately and threatened him not to speak about what he had seen.

Just a few hours before the Silva sisters' encounter, a married couple living near the town reported seeing an unidentified craft flying erratically through the sky. Like Carlos, they noted that the craft appeared damaged and was trailing smoke as it descended toward the city. Not long after, residents in the Jardim Andere neighborhood began calling the police, reporting that a strange animal had been seen running through the streets. A construction worker later claimed that he saw local police corner the creature, trap it in a wooden box, and drive away.

At around 1:00 p.m., several Varginha residents reported seeing men in military uniforms combing through the town, seemingly searching for something. Their movements were calculated and intense, as if they were on a mission. Some locals even claimed to have heard gunshots echoing through the streets, raising fears that whatever they were looking for was dangerous—or possibly not of this world. Just two hours after the military presence was first noticed, the Silva sisters and Kátia Andrade allegedly came face-to-face with the strange creature crouching in the weeds.

Around 5:30 p.m., twenty-three-year-old military police officer Marco Eli Chereze came across one of the creatures after hearing reports about it in the vacant lot. According to multiple reports, Officer Chereze approached and captured the creature with his bare hands. It's said the creature's skin felt slimy and cold, and it emitted a pungent, sulfur-like smell that made Marco's eyes water. Despite his discomfort, he managed to place the creature in the back seat of his patrol car and drove it to the nearest hospital. Hospital staff later denied ever seeing the creature, but several witnesses claim that it died later that night under highly mysterious circumstances. The body was then allegedly loaded onto a truck and transported to the Escola de Sargentos das Armas (Weapons Sergeant School) for examination under strict military supervision.

Later, workers from another hospital, the nearby Humanitas Hospital, came forward, claiming that military officers brought in a strange, humanoid figure on the same day. The figure was alive but barely moving—its skin was brown and wet-looking, and it had large, red eyes. One doctor allegedly tried to examine it, but the military quickly intervened and removed the body. According to some reports, the creature died later that day, and its body was immediately taken away by government officials.

Three days later, on January 23, several witnesses reported seeing a military convoy leaving Varginha under heavy guard. It was rumored that the convoy was transporting the bodies of multiple extraterrestrials that had been recovered from the crash site and surrounding area. The Brazilian government, however, firmly denied these claims, insisting that no such event had taken place.

Then, on February 7, just a few weeks after Officer Chereze's encounter, he was rushed to the hospital after experiencing intense pain in his arm, along with partial paralysis. Medical staff were baffled—his condition deteriorated rapidly, and they discovered a large abscess under his armpit. Surgeons attempted to remove the infected tissue, but Marco's health continued to decline. He developed a severe fever and showed signs of organ failure. Despite the hospital's best efforts, Marco died shortly after the surgery. Doctors were at a loss to explain the cause of death, as Marco's symptoms resembled no known illness or infection.

Rumors immediately spread that Marco's mysterious illness was directly connected to his contact with the alien. Witnesses recalled that Marco wrestled the creature barehanded, and some speculated that he may have been exposed to an alien bacterium or virus—something his immune system simply couldn't fight off. In the end, the military refused to release any medical reports or autopsy details.

Marco's body was also allegedly removed from the hospital under military escort and buried under strict secrecy. His family was given little information about what had happened to him, and authorities refused to comment on whether his death was linked to the Varginha incident.

The Brazilian government has consistently denied any involvement in the Varginha incident, including any effort to cover up what happened on January 20, 1996. Officials attributed the sightings and strange occurrences to a combination of misidentified wildlife, unusual weather conditions, and collective hysteria. They insisted there was no alien encounter, no crashed UFO, and certainly no cover-up. However, several inconsistencies have been cited in the government's responses. Their explanation that the creatures were deformed animals was quickly debunked by local veterinarians, who stated that no known species matched the description given by the eyewitnesses. Furthermore, the government's claim that the military presence in Varginha that day was part of a routine training exercise doesn't hold up under scrutiny. Witnesses reported seeing armed soldiers, helicopters, and even plain-clothed agents securing the crash site and transporting debris. The area where the supposed crash occurred was also quickly sealed off and remains restricted to this day—a move that many believe was designed to prevent any independent investigation or evidence recovery.

But most people found it hard to dismiss the sheer number of credible eyewitnesses, the recurrent details across individual testimonies, and the alleged physical evidence. There were also the detailed accounts of the Silva sisters and Kátia Andrade Xavier, the claims of construction workers who saw the creature captured by the police, the sightings of military personnel moving in and out of the town with unmarked vehicles, and the death of Officer Marco Eli Chereze shortly after handling the creature. Some theorists believe that the alien (or aliens) were transported to a secret facility, possibly with the assistance of the U.S. government, to be studied and kept hidden from the public.

Despite being such a well-documented case with multiple eyewitnesses, the Varginha Alien incident remains shrouded in government secrecy to this day. For many, that's proof enough that the truth is being hidden.

THE BLACK-EYED KIDS

MULTIPLE LOCATIONS AND INCIDENTS

You may have heard whispers of the black-eyed children, a chilling legend that has haunted countless people across the world for years. These strange and unsettling beings have been described by many as either demons or extraterrestrial entities—yet no one truly knows what they are or where they come from.

While they may first appear to look like ordinary children or teenagers, the black-eyed children possess disturbing features—deathly pale skin, outdated or ill-fitting clothing, and, most unsettling, solid black eyes that seem devoid of any soul or emotion. Despite their strange appearances, they always behave in a calm and calculated manner. Witnesses often say these children will appear out of nowhere—usually at night—and approach unsuspecting people with strange requests. They will ask to be let into homes, cars, or other places of safety, claiming they need to use the phone, get out of the cold, or find their parents. But no matter how innocent their requests may seem, there is one rule that must be followed: Never let them in.

Of course, the black-eyed children are terrifyingly persistent. They will knock on doors, tap on windows, and stand completely still for long periods, waiting to be acknowledged. Their voices are monotonous and unsettling, as if they are forcing themselves to mimic human speech.

Those who have ignored this warning, allowing the black-eyed children into their safe spaces, have suffered terrifying consequences: sudden streaks of bad luck, unexplained illnesses, and even the untimely deaths of family members and pets. Some victims claim that after an encounter, they experienced strange hallucinations, overwhelming dread, or a lingering sickness that doctors couldn't explain. Others report electrical disturbances, shadowy figures lurking in their homes, or a suffocating sense of paranoia that never quite fades. Some believe they are soul-stealing entities that feed off human fear. Others speculate they are alien hybrids sent to observe us.

One woman, who shared her experience anonymously, recounted being in bed alongside her husband and their toddler when their three-month-old puppy, usually playful and innocent, had become unnervingly still. The puppy was fixated on the front door as if sensing an unseen presence outside. At first, the woman brushed off the dog's behavior as simple curiosity, but seeing its posture—rigid and alert—made her uneasy.

She finally decided to show the dog that there was nothing to fear. As she approached the door, she noticed the puppy's hackles rise and its growl morph into something she had never heard before—low, guttural, and filled with rage. It was an aggressive, almost primal sound, the kind of growl that warned of imminent danger. Her hand moved toward the dead bolt, but before she could turn it, the dog's demeanor shifted. The violent growling ceased, replaced by trembling, whimpering fear. A cold wave of dread washed over the woman, a feeling so intense it rooted her in place. It was as if an invisible force was warning her not to open the door.

Her pulse quickened as she hesitantly leaned forward, pressing her eye against the peephole. She saw two figures standing on the porch, motionless. One was a teenage girl with long, stringy blond hair that partially obscured her face. She was slender, almost unnaturally so, and wore an olive-colored pullover hoodie with faded jeans. In her hand, she clutched the fingers of a much smaller girl—no older than three or four. The younger child mirrored the older one's unsettling features: pale skin, thin frame, and an unnatural stillness. Her head was tilted downward; her gaze locked onto the ground.

Under any other circumstances, the woman might have opened the door without hesitation, offering the children warmth, food, or a phone to call their parents. But this was different. Every fiber of her being screamed that something was wrong.

Then the older girl spoke: "We have to use your phone." Her voice was confident and composed. The woman felt her breath hitch. The girl never lifted her head, never looked up, yet somehow, she knew someone was behind the door. The woman hadn't turned on any lights, hadn't made a sound—how did they know she was there? She remained silent, frozen in place. Then, with unnerving precision, the older child tilted her head upward, revealing her eyes—two voids of pure black. No whites, no irises, just endless darkness, like a hole in the universe itself. "Our mother is worried," she said flatly.

The woman's grip on the doorknob tightened as a realization struck her—only a thin wooden door separated her from whatever stood outside. Her body urged her to move, to retreat, yet something deep inside—a strange, almost magnetic pull—urged her to stay, to listen, to let them in. But she didn't. She took a single step backward.

The girl's expression didn't change, but her tone did. What had been polite before now carried an edge of frustration. "Just let us in to use your phone," she insisted. Another step back. And then the girl's demeanor shifted entirely. The false sweetness drained from her voice, replaced by a harsh, ugly tone. "We're not going to hurt you. If we wanted to, we would have broken in."

The woman's chest tightened as an invisible force pulled her toward the door, urging her to unlock it. It wasn't a physical pull—no hands, no force—but a mental compulsion, an unnatural persuasion gnawing at her thoughts, whispering to let them in. Somehow she resisted. She turned and fled back to her bedroom, slamming the door shut and pulling the curtains over the windows. But even then, the children didn't leave. Their voices, insistent, continued to call out to her through the night, their requests turning into demands. She never slept that night. In fact, she's never truly slept well since.

Another encounter, on March 17, 2008, involved a thirteen-year-old boy, who was sitting in an old Chevy pickup truck, waiting for his mother to finish her haircut inside a local hairdresser. The night was quiet, and at first, everything seemed normal. About fifteen minutes had passed when he noticed a boy pacing back and forth along the sidewalk in front of the parked truck. Something about the boy's posture and slow, deliberate movements caught his attention. For a moment, he thought he recognized him as a friend from school, so he knocked on the window, trying to get his attention.

But as soon as the boy turned and approached the truck, a wave of unease crept in. The boy in the truck didn't recognize him at all. Still, he felt no immediate fear—just confusion. The strange boy walked up to the driver's side window and stood completely still, staring. The silence stretched uncomfortably. Then, the boy inside the truck saw his eyes. They were completely black—pure darkness.

And then, in a hushed, almost hypnotic whisper, the boy outside spoke: "You must let me in." Panic surged through the boy's body. He let out a bloodcurdling scream, his hands fumbling for the locks as he quickly secured every door. Without another thought, he dove down into the footwell, his heart hammering against his ribs. He squeezed his eyes shut and forced himself to stay silent, every second stretching into eternity. Minutes passed—five in total—before he finally gathered the courage to peek over the dashboard. The black-eyed child was gone.

The boy was flooded with relief, but it was short-lived. When his mother finally returned to the car, she looked unsettled. Before he could tell her what had happened, she spoke. She told him that a boy had entered the hair salon while she was inside. A boy with pitch-black eyes. He had approached her with an odd calmness and insisted—demanded—that she hand over her car keys. Thankfully, she refused. Because if she hadn't, her son might not have been there to tell the story.

The origins of the black-eyed children are just as mysterious as the entities themselves. Many believe their presence dates back centuries, with legends of similar beings appearing in folklore and mythology across different cultures. Stories of dark-eyed supernatural figures have long been associated with omens of misfortune, death, and other unsettling events. Some ancient tales describe wandering spirits or demonic entities that take the form of children to lure unsuspecting victims into danger. Others suggest they are shape-shifters, using their youthful appearance to manipulate and deceive.

Some believe the black-eyed children are extraterrestrial beings or interdimensional entities, their black eyes a reflection of something inhuman. Others claim they are demonic figures, seeking permission to enter homes or vehicles to bring chaos and suffering to those who let them in. Despite countless reported encounters, no definitive proof of their existence has ever been found. Paranormal researchers and enthusiasts continue to investigate, hoping to uncover the truth behind these mysterious entities.

One thing is known: The black-eyed children cannot enter your home, car, or wherever you are without permission. But that does little to ease the terror of coming face-to-face with them, standing on your doorstep, waiting patiently for you to give in. Do not speak to them, do not acknowledge them, and whatever you do, never let them in.

THE ALIEN SUICIDE

AN UNDISCLOSED LOCATION IN THE UNITED STATES

2012

A truck driver named Scott Murray and his wife, Elizabeth, had built a quiet and fulfilling life together. Their three children had grown up, moved out, and started families of their own. Though Scott's job kept him away from home for long stretches at a time, he always found comfort in knowing Elizabeth was safe in their house, waiting for his return.

Then one night, while on a long-haul job in Michigan, Scott received a frantic call from Elizabeth. Her voice trembled, her words barely coherent as she struggled to explain what had happened. She told him she believed she had been drugged, possibly assaulted—maybe even raped. The sheer terror in her voice sent Scott into a panic. He immediately urged her to call the police, but she refused. Something in her tone suggested she wasn't just scared—she was utterly disturbed. Desperate to reach her and uncover the truth, Scott turned his truck around and sped home as fast as he could.

When he finally arrived home, he found Elizabeth in a state of utter distress, her hands shaking, her face pale, her eyes darting around as if she expected something—or someone—to be watching. He pressed her to tell him what had happened, but she hesitated, as if she didn't know how to say the words. When she finally spoke, her answer left him speechless. She told him she hadn't been attacked by a person—she believed she'd been abducted by something not of this world.

Scott's initial reaction was disbelief. His mind raced for a rational explanation—perhaps she had suffered a vivid nightmare, or the

trauma had left her confused. But the fear in her eyes was undeniable, and when he noticed how she flinched at every shadow and sound, he knew something deeply disturbing had occurred. Determined to get to the bottom of it, he took her to the emergency room. Doctors found no signs of physical assault, yet they did discover something distressing—an unusual burn mark on her right shoulder. It wasn't a bruise, nor did it resemble anything that could be easily explained. The doctors had no answers, leaving Scott even more unsettled.

Hoping that rest would bring her clarity, Scott brought Elizabeth home, praying that by morning, things would return to normal. But when he stepped outside the next day, he was stopped in his tracks. Four large, circular burn marks scarred their lawn, each one perfectly shaped and brittle to the touch. A section of their wooden stockade fence had been scorched—and, even stranger, about twenty feet up in a nearby tree, a cluster of leaves had been burned, yet were still clinging to the branches.

Scott scanned the horizon, searching for an explanation, but their home was miles away from the nearest neighbor. There was no one to ask if they had seen anything unusual. Elizabeth, however, was growing more terrified by the hour. The fear in her eyes deepened, and despite Scott's efforts to comfort her, she barely spoke.

It wasn't until Elizabeth underwent hypnotic regression that the full horror of her experience was revealed. In her hypnotized state, she recalled floating from the exact spot where the burn marks now scorched the ground, lifted effortlessly into the air by an invisible power. The next thing she remembered was being inside a metallic, dimly lit space—cold, sterile, and utterly alien. Shadowy figures surrounded her, their features indistinct, their hands moving with precise, methodical intent. She described terrifying procedures being performed on her, each more invasive than the last. There was no pain—only an overwhelming sense of helplessness and dread.

The memories shattered her. Scott, a man who had always relied on logic and reason, found himself caught between disbelief and an inescapable truth—something had happened to his wife. Whether it was an abduction, an experiment, or something beyond human understanding, he could no longer deny that the scars on their land—and on Elizabeth's mind—were real.

A week later, Scott returned to work, attempting to resume a sense of normalcy after the harrowing events that had upended his life. But while he was back on the road, tragedy struck again. Overwhelmed by the trauma of her experience and the weight of an unspeakable fear, Elizabeth took her own life. The very gun Scott had given her for protection had become the tool of her despair.

The loss was devastating. The woman he had loved for decades—the one he had built a life with—was gone, and Scott was left with nothing but grief and unanswered questions. He refused to believe that Elizabeth had simply lost her mind. She had never been suicidal, had never shown signs of mental distress before that night. Whatever had happened to her had shattered her so completely that she saw no way forward. Scott couldn't accept that the truth would die with her.

Determined to find answers, he reached out to countless researchers, investigators, and UFO experts. He poured himself into the search, desperate to prove that Elizabeth's abduction—and the horrors she claimed to have endured—were not just the figments of a disturbed mind. He sent multiple samples of their burned grass to a university for testing, hoping for scientific validation. The initial results were shocking—they came back with traces of radiation exposure. It was the first concrete piece of evidence that something truly unexplainable had occurred that night.

But then, without explanation, the results were retracted, and no further reports were released. It was as if someone—or something—had intervened, ensuring that whatever had been found would never see the light of day. The abrupt reversal only fueled Scott's suspicions.

Despite numerous setbacks, Scott plans to keep Elizabeth's story alive. More than anything, he wants justice for Elizabeth. He wants people to understand that whatever she encountered—whatever abducted and assaulted her—left her so broken that she saw no escape other than death.

Some believe that Elizabeth was a tragic victim of extraterrestrial experimentation, part of a pattern of abductions that have spanned decades. Others suspect government interference, a cover-up designed to keep humanity blind to the presence of beings that operate in the shadows. To this day, no definitive answers have emerged. The events of that night remain shrouded in uncertainty, leaving behind only fear, grief, and unanswered questions.

One thing remains certain—whatever happened to Elizabeth Murray that night changed her forever, leading to an end so devastating that Scott has spent every moment since searching for the truth.

THE BLOND ALIEN WOMAN

SYDNEY, AUSTRALIA
1988

In 1973, Peter Khoury, originally from Lebanon, moved to Australia, where he met his future wife, Vivian. The couple were high school sweethearts and led a normal, happy life. In February 1988, while in Sydney, Peter and Vivian witnessed a bright white object in the sky, followed by strange, erratic beams of light. At the time, they thought it was peculiar but quickly brushed it off. However, while living with family that summer, Peter was abruptly jolted awake by an unseen force grabbing his ankle. A wave of paralysis washed over his body, leaving him conscious but completely immobilized. As panic set in, Peter noticed four hooded figures standing around his bed. They were small, no more than three or four feet tall. Their faces were obscured by the shadows of their hoods, yet their presence radiated an undeniable sense of power and control.

Then a taller being emerged, a thin, humanoid figure with enormous black eyes, its elongated form draped in a strange yellow suit. The entities communicated telepathically, instructing Peter to relax. Despite their seemingly calm directive, he remained terrified. As he watched helplessly, one of the figures produced a long, metallic needle and brought it toward his head. Before he could process what was happening, darkness consumed him.

When Peter finally regained consciousness, he was still in bed, but something felt profoundly wrong. He bolted upright and rushed into the living room, hoping to get answers from his father and brother, who were sleeping there. He struggled to wake them up, and when his brother finally woke up, he said he felt "switched off." Then Peter noticed the time—what felt like mere minutes had actually been over an hour, leading him to believe his family had been sedated by the entities. Peter was left with a puncture mark surrounded by dried blood on his head, surgical-like scars on his legs, and an unsettling void in his memory, unable to recall what had transpired after the needle was inserted. He was also completely paralyzed by fear, unsure of what to do or how to make sense of what had happened. With little to no knowledge about extraterrestrial phenomena, Peter found himself spiraling, struggling to comprehend what he had experienced.

Over time, however, he began researching similar cases and immersed himself in the world of ufology. Driven by a need for answers and connection, he founded the UFO Experience Support Association (UFOESA)—a group dedicated to helping others who had alien encounters. Peter became a source of support for fellow experiencers, but despite his growing understanding of the phenomenon, his own encounters were far from over.

In 1992, Peter experienced an even more disturbing—and deeply personal encounter—one he would hesitate to speak about for years due to its highly sexual nature.

After dropping Vivian off at the train station one night, Peter went home and, exhausted from being ill, he went straight to bed and quickly fell asleep. He was woken by the feeling of the mattress sinking beneath him, and when he opened his eyes, he was shocked to find two naked humanoid females sitting on the edge of his bed, watching him. To Peter, they were unmistakably alien. Their dark eyes were double the size of an average person and their faces were elongated in an unnatural way. The blond female, who had long, almost translucent hair, exuded an unnerving presence. Before Peter could react, she suddenly reached forward, grabbing the back of his head with incredible strength and pulling him toward her bare chest.

A wave of panic surged through him as he struggled to break free, but her grip was unrelenting. Peter did the only thing he could think of—he bit her nipple, hard. To his horror, he felt a small fragment break off into his mouth. Yet the blond woman showed no reaction—no pain, no scream, nothing. Shocked and choking, Peter accidentally swallowed the small piece before being overcome by a violent coughing fit. When he finally recovered, he looked up—and the two women were gone. They had vanished as suddenly as they had appeared.

Shaken and bewildered, Peter soon noticed his genitals were in excruciating pain, as if they were being constricted. When he checked, he found two thin strands of blond hair tightly wrapped around his penis. As he carefully unwound them, he struggled to process what had just happened. He instinctively placed the strands of hair into a small plastic bag—preserving what would become the most crucial piece of physical evidence in an alien encounter ever recorded.

It wouldn't be until 1996, when he met a leading Australian UFO researcher, Bill Chalker, that Peter finally revealed the harrowing details of his encounter. With the help of Bill, he also submitted the blond strands of hair for analysis, hoping that science could shed light on his terrifying experience. The hair was sent to scientists from the Anomaly Physical Evidence Group (APEG), a team dedicated to investigating unexplained biological samples. At first glance, the hair appeared to be entirely human—something that initially seemed to debunk the notion of extraterrestrial involvement. However, upon closer examination, researchers found that the hair contained five distinct DNA markers that are most commonly found in people of East Asian or Indigenous North American descent. Further studies revealed that, at the time, only four known living women on Earth possessed all five of these rare DNA markers. They were all of Chinese descent, with naturally black hair. But the hair in question was blond, fine, and almost translucent. This baffling contradiction left scientists at a dead end. Despite extensive research, no conclusive answers have ever been found regarding the origins of the mysterious hair—or, more disturbingly, the nature of Peter's encounter. For Peter, there is no room for doubt. The memories of that night are etched into his mind, as vivid and unsettling as the moment they occurred. He remains deeply haunted by the experience, convinced that the blond beings were not a hallucination, a dream, or a fabrication, but a terrifying reality.

The case of Peter Khoury is one of the most extraordinary alien abduction cases in history, as it remains the first documented incident where an alleged extraterrestrial specimen was recovered from a human body and later subjected to DNA testing. And yet the ultimate truth remains just out of reach, leaving Peter and the rest of the world grappling with an enigma that may never be solved.

THE MEN IN BLACK COME TO VISIT

OLD ORCHARD BEACH, MAINE

1976

On the evening of September 11, 1976, Dr. Herbert Hopkins sat quietly, enjoying a rare moment of solitude in his home near Maine's Old Orchard Beach. His wife and children were away for the evening, and the house was unusually quiet. The salty breeze from the Atlantic drifted through the open window, mingling with the scent of old books and the faint hum of a tape recorder. At fifty-eight years old, Dr. Hopkins was a respected allergist and researcher whose work on multiple sclerosis had earned him a reputation for methodical, scientific rigor. Yet, over the past few weeks, his thoughts had strayed far from the confines of medical science. For some time now, he had been delving into the otherworldly—conducting hypnosis sessions with David Stephens, a man who claimed to have been abducted by aliens in Oxford, Maine, in 1975. The case was unlike anything Dr. Hopkins had come across before. Stephens's vivid recollections painted unsettling images of mushroom-headed entities with inky, unblinking eyes inside an unearthly craft. Hopkins found himself repeatedly playing the tapes, dissecting every pause, every whispered fear, searching for the rational explanation his scientific mind craved. But the more he analyzed, the more elusive the truth became. Was it a psychological episode, a shared delusion, or was it something science couldn't explain? These questions gnawed at him, keeping him awake at night.

A jarring ring of the telephone snapped Dr. Hopkins out of focus. He reached for the receiver, expecting a wrong number, but instead, a flat, emotionless voice introduced itself as the vice president of the New Jersey UFO Research Organization. They claimed to be calling from a nearby phone booth and expressed a desire to discuss Dr. Hopkins's recent work on the Stephens case. Intrigued by the chance to exchange theories with another researcher, Hopkins agreed and provided his address. As he hung up, he flipped on the porch light, but before his finger even left the switch, a dark figure was already approaching—ascending the steps of the porch with an eerily smooth stride. A cold wave of dread washed over Hopkins. The nearest phone booth was several blocks away. There was simply no way the man could have arrived so quickly. Yet there he stood, tall and imposing, dressed in a flawless black suit that seemed to absorb the light around him. A black fedora sat low on his head, and his skin was a pale, waxy texture. The figure's lips stretched unnaturally into a cold smile. Hopkins's pulse quickened as he realized that despite the warmth of the night, the man wore thick gloves.

Hesitant but compelled, Hopkins opened the door, and in that instant, he unwittingly welcomed the strangest visitor he would ever encounter—one of the men in black. The visitor stepped over the threshold with a stiff, unnatural gait, his glossy black shoes whispering against the hardwood floor. He removed his black fedora with a deliberate, mechanical motion to reveal a perfectly smooth, bald head—unusually reflective under the living room light. The man's face was utterly devoid of hair—no eyebrows, no eyelashes—nothing to break the unsettlingly smooth surface of his pale, almost translucent skin. The only hint of color on his face was his unnaturally red lips, vivid and glossy, as if painted on. Hopkins couldn't help but think the man looked artificial, more like a wax mannequin than a living, breathing human.

Dr. Hopkins gestured toward the living room and invited the stranger to sit. The man lowered himself rigidly into a chair opposite the doctor, folding his gloved hands neatly in his lap. Despite the man's unsettling appearance, Hopkins pushed forward, driven by a lingering curiosity about his unexpected guest. The stranger immediately began asking questions about the hypnosis sessions, his voice a flat monotone with an unnatural cadence, each word pronounced with the cold precision of a machine. Hopkins answered, but a prickling sense of dread crept over as the man's questions were becoming alarmingly specific, probing into details of the Stephens case that only someone deeply involved could possibly know. "Yes, that's the way I understand it," the man would respond with an emotionless nod after each of Hopkins's answers, his gaze never wavering. Hopkins felt increasingly scrutinized, the cold eyes of the visitor boring into him—a man whose name he didn't even know. Despite the introduction over the phone, the visitor had never identified himself. The omission now felt intentional, as if the stranger's very presence was a deliberate intrusion.

Before Hopkins could say anything, the man raised a gloved hand to his red-lipped mouth and accidentally brushed it against them. To Hopkins's horror, a smear of red lipstick stained the glove's gray surface, revealing that there were no lips at all. The vibrant red was nothing more than a cosmetic deception, concealing a featureless void beneath. The stranger, unfazed by the slip, leaned forward and pointed a gloved finger at Hopkins's pocket. In that same cold, detached tone, he stated, "You have two coins in your pocket." Hopkins blinked, stunned. He did, in fact, have two coins—an innocuous detail known only to him. The man instructed him to remove one of the coins and hold it in his palm.

Nervously, Hopkins complied, reaching into his pocket and pulling out a shiny copper penny. He placed it in his open palm, the coin's surface catching the light as it rested there. The stranger leaned closer, his gaze intent. Hopkins's hand trembled, a creeping fear telling him he was in the presence of something not of this Earth.

"Watch the coin," the strange man instructed. As Hopkins stared at the copper penny, the light in the room seemed to dim, and Hopkins's vision blurred as if he were drifting into a trance. The coin's color began to shift, rippling with iridescent hues before vanishing. The skin on his palm tingled where the coin had been moments before. Hopkins blinked hard, but the penny was gone. "Nobody on this plane will ever see that coin again," the man stated. Hopkins's mind reeled as he struggled to comprehend what had just happened.

Then, without warning, the man abruptly shifted the conversation. "Do you know what happened to Barney Hill?" he asked, emotionless. Hopkins hesitated.

The case of Betty and Barney Hill—the first widely publicized alien abduction in the United States—was well-known to him. "I don't, except that he died," he replied cautiously.

"Do you know what he died from?" the man pressed.

"A heart attack, maybe?" Hopkins ventured, though he wasn't certain.

"No," the strange man said, the word heavy and ominous. "That's not accurate. He died because he knew too much." His response lingered in the air, sharp and foreboding. Hopkins quickly realized the veiled warning behind the words—an unspoken threat that made his blood run cold.

The man slowly rose and turned toward the door, pausing for a moment. "My energy is running low. Must go. Goodbye," he mumbled, his voice distorted. He shuffled awkwardly toward the door, limbs moving in a stilted, unnatural manner. Hopkins sat frozen, pulse hammering in his ears. He was too stunned to speak, too terrified to move.

As the man exited, Hopkins rushed to the door, desperate to catch one last glimpse of his bizarre visitor. But when he peered outside, he saw nothing but blinding blue lights bathing the driveway—pulsing, intense, and otherworldly. The lights quickly vanished, leaving Hopkins clutching the doorframe. The man's cryptic warning about Barney Hill gnawed at him, unable to shake the feeling that the strange visitor's appearance had been a dire warning—one aimed directly at him.

In the days that followed, Hopkins began to question every shadow, every noise, and every flicker of movement just beyond his vision. He was confident that the encounter was a threat: Stop your research. Walk away. Forget what you've seen. With trembling hands,

Hopkins erased all the hypnosis tapes, destroying any evidence of his work. He abandoned the UFO abduction case completely, distancing himself from the paranormal and severing ties with the investigation. Later, Hopkins would discover that no record of the New Jersey UFO Research Organization could be found—it simply didn't exist. The encounter forever haunted him, and he was left with a deep, gnawing fear that he had brushed against a hidden truth—something far more dangerous and incomprehensible than he could have imagined.

The 1976 Herbert Hopkins case remains one of the most detailed and compelling accounts of an encounter with the men in black—enigmatic figures often described as agents of suppression, silencing witnesses and erasing evidence of extraterrestrial encounters. Their origins are as murky as their intentions, and those who have crossed paths with them speak of an unshakable, primal fear—a sense that something profoundly wrong lurks beneath their unnatural facade. Those who study the phenomenon often cite Hopkins's case as a cornerstone of the men in black mystery. Decades later, the question remains: Who—or what—are the men in black, and what are they so desperate to keep hidden?

CHAPTER FOUR

THE HUNTED

Murders, Cold Cases, and Other Tales of True Crime and Terror

A REAL-LIFE HORROR MOVIE

POCATELLO, IDAHO

2006

Cassie Jo Stoddart was a responsible straight-A student from Pocatello, Idaho. To her friends and family, she was also kind, ambitious, artistic, and easy to love. So, when her aunt and uncle, Allison and Frank Contreras, were heading out of town for a weekend trip, they asked sixteen-year-old Cassie to care for their home and pets, which was only a few miles away from Cassie's own home. On the night of September 22, 2006, Cassie arrived, eager to spend time at her aunt and uncle's home and happy to help them out.

As the night went on, Cassie grew bored and decided to invite her boyfriend, Matt Beckham, over to keep her company. Matt, in turn, brought his friend Torey Adamcik, who invited Brian Draper. Cassie was familiar with the two boys. That same morning, they were going around school with a video camera and had recorded her at her locker.

When Torey and Brian arrived, Cassie gave them a brief tour of the house, including the basement. After the tour, the four teens sat down to watch *Kill Bill: Vol. 2*, but before the movie was over, Torey and Brian decided to leave, claiming they'd rather watch something at the movie theater. But before leaving, Brian unlocked the basement door, ensuring they could return undetected.

Later that night, Torey and Brian returned to the neighborhood, parking their car down the street. Dressed in dark clothing, gloves, and red-and-white painted masks, they quietly entered the house through the unlocked basement door. They started making loud noises from the basement, hoping to lure Cassie and Matt from upstairs, where they were still watching a movie. But to their surprise, the couple didn't notice. Next, they turned their attention to the circuit breaker, shutting off all the power in the house. Still, the couple remained undeterred. Frustrated, Torey and Brian began flipping a few lights back on.

Upstairs, Cassie started to feel uneasy from the lights flickering on and off. Adding to her discomfort, the family dog stood at the top of the basement stairs, barking and growling. Matt, noticing that Cassie was on edge, called his mother to ask if he could stay the night and keep her company. His mother refused but offered to let Cassie stay at their house, promising to take her back in the morning. However, Cassie declined, feeling it was her duty to care for her aunt and uncle's house and their animals. Around 10:30 p.m., Matt's mother picked him up, leaving Cassie alone.

On his way home, Matt called Torey, asking if he and Brian wanted to meet up. Torey spoke in a low tone that made it hard for Matt to understand him, so Matt assumed they were still at the movies. Confident that Matt was gone, Torey and Brian turned the circuit breaker off again. Cassie stayed put. Realizing she wouldn't come down to the basement, they crept upstairs, slamming a closet door to frighten her. Cassie, who was drifting off to sleep, was startled but didn't investigate.

Realizing their scare tactics weren't going to lure Cassie, the boys decided to ambush her. Armed with weapons—Brian holding a daggerlike blade and Torey a hunting knife—and fueled by adrenaline, they stabbed Cassie relentlessly. She was struck thirty times; twelve of the wounds were fatal. As she screamed in agony, blood splattering across the room, Torey and Brian fled the scene, leaving Cassie to bleed out alone in the dark.

As Torey and Brian scrambled into their car, they recorded their thoughts on a camcorder. "We just killed Cassie," Torey said, his voice trembling with excitement and exhilaration. "We just left her house. This is not a joke. I stabbed her in the throat and saw her lifeless body just disappear, dude," he continued. Beside him, Brian appeared more subdued, his face revealing hints of fear and regret, as though the gravity of what he'd done was beginning to sink in. Torey, however, had his ego inflated when he met up with Matt the next day. He reveled in his friend's growing concern as he desperately tried to reach Cassie.

Cassie's body wasn't discovered until two days after her murder, when her aunt and uncle returned from their trip. The scene was horrific—her blood-soaked corpse covered with countless stab wounds and lacerations. When officers finally arrived, they described it as one of the most brutal and heartbreaking cases they'd ever encountered. A full-scale investigation was launched immediately.

Police initially focused on Matt's mother's boyfriend, whose fingerprints were found on the circuit breaker in the basement. During questioning, he told them that he had done work on the property months prior. The Contreras family confirmed this, and he was no longer a suspect. The next obvious lead was Matt himself, since he was the last person to see her alive. While being interrogated, Matt told investigators about the entire night: hanging out with Torey and Brian, the strange flickering of the lights, and being picked up by his mom. His mom corroborated his story, adding that she heard Cassie's voice when she picked Matt up—proof Cassie was alive when they left. Matt also passed a polygraph test, convincing police he was not Cassie's murderer. Now aware there had been two other friends at the house, the police brought Torey and Brian in for questioning.

Torey told police that he and Brian arrived at the Contreras house around 8:30 p.m. expecting a party. When they realized there was no party, they left and decided to catch a movie. The police then pressed both boys for details about the movie they supposedly went to see, but both Torey and Brian failed to recall any, which immediately raised red flags. Sensing they were being lied to, detectives pressed harder. Brian eventually cracked and confessed to Cassie's murder—significantly downplaying his role and shifting much of the blame onto Torey. Brian admitted he was in the same room as Torey during Cassie's murder but initially denied stabbing her. In later interrogations, however, he confessed to stabbing her under Torey's command, claiming Torey had told him to "make sure she's dead."

Three days later, Brian led investigators to Black Rock Canyon, where he and Torey had attempted to destroy and bury their evidence. At the site, police recovered their clothes, boots, red-and-white masks, latex gloves, and murder weapons. They also found the camera and videotape the boys used the day of Cassie's murder. They had tried to burn the videotape, but the police were able to salvage it, revealing both their premeditated plans and disturbing reactions: exhilaration and callousness.

The trial was grueling, including both a reading of the videotape's transcript as well as the footage of Torey and Brian laughing and bragging about murdering Cassie. The prosecution also revealed that the teens idolized the Columbine High School shooters and were obsessed with—even fixated on—the *Scream* horror franchise, in which high school students murder their friends. The two teens dreamed of becoming infamous killers, even creating a kill list, with Cassie at the very top.

Despite their attempts to shift blame onto one another, both Torey and Brian were convicted of first-degree murder and conspiracy to commit murder. They both received mandatory life sentences without the possibility of parole, along with an additional thirty years to life for conspiracy. Torey and Brian robbed Cassie of her future, and the impact of their crime has forever changed her family and her community.

THE BASEMENT OF HORROR

INDIANAPOLIS, INDIANA
1965

Sylvia Likens was a sweet, kindhearted girl from Indiana with a bright smile and lively spirit. She was one of five children: Diana, Daniel, Sylvia, Jenny, and Benjamin, a.k.a. "Benny." While Sylvia cared for all her siblings, she had an unbreakable bond with her younger sister, Jenny. Her parents, Lester and Elizabeth "Betty" Likens, were carnival workers—constantly traveling, struggling to make ends meet, and often facing difficult decisions.

In July 1965, when Sylvia was sixteen years old, her father had yet another difficult decision to make. Her mother was serving time in jail for shoplifting, and Lester had to return to their carnival concession business. He desperately needed someone to care for Sylvia and Jenny. Diana was married and living independently, while Danny and Benny were able to stay with their grandparents.

Lester turned to a family acquaintance, Gertrude Baniszewski, a single mother of seven children, who was equally impoverished and overwhelmed. Despite her own struggles—including a history of failed marriages, severe depression, and a reliance on prescription drugs—Gertrude agreed to take in the girls for twenty dollars a week. Though she was far from an ideal caregiver, Lester felt he had no other choice. When he dropped Sylvia and Jenny off, he reportedly told Gertrude to "straighten his daughters out." The first few days went well at the Baniszewski house; however, Sylvia often clashed with Gertrude's oldest daughter, Paula, who was resentful and jealous of Sylvia's youth, beauty, and potential—qualities Paula felt she lacked.

Then, about two weeks into their arrangement, Lester was late on a payment and continued to deliver payments irregularly, often days behind. After this, Gertrude's mood shifted dramatically, and she focused her anger on the sisters. She started using a quarter-inch-thick paddle to beat Sylvia and Jenny on their buttocks, yelling, "I took care of you two bitches for two weeks for nothing!" As time went on, and Lester continued to be late on his payments, Gertrude's rage escalated. On one occasion, both girls were struck approximately fifteen times on their backs after Paula accused them of eating too much at a church supper. When Gertrude, frail and exhausted, could no longer wield the paddle herself, she handed it to Paula, who eagerly continued the beatings in her place.

As time went on, Gertrude started focusing her abuse on Sylvia—fueled by jealousy, the same resentment harbored by her daughter Paula. She even forced Jenny to participate in the violence, threatening that if she refused, she would face similar punishments. Sylvia's abuse started out with a combination of starvation and beatings but quickly escalated to more degrading acts. Gertrude forced Sylvia to eat leftover spoiled food, even rotten scraps pulled from the trash. She burned Sylvia's fingertips for allegedly stealing. At a church function, she force-fed her hot dogs covered in condiments until she vomited. When Sylvia threw up, Gertrude's punishment was even more dehumanizing—she forced Sylvia to eat her own vomit for "wasting food."

Eventually, Gertrude began encouraging all her children to partake in abusing Sylvia. The children started practicing their karate on Sylvia, slamming her on the floor or against the walls. They tossed her down the stairs. They would cut open her skin, rubbing salt into her open wounds. They would also "cleanse" Sylvia by putting her in a scalding hot bath. Paula, herself pregnant at the time, accused Sylvia of being pregnant to make fun of her weight. Paula would also stomp on Sylvia's vagina and call her a whore. One day, Paula beat Sylvia with such force that she broke her own wrist and needed a cast. She then used her cast to further beat Sylvia. Gertrude's son John Jr. made Sylvia lick his one-year-old brother's urine- and feces-filled diapers clean.

Sylvia, seeking revenge, started a rumor at Arsenal Technical High School that Gertrude and her daughter Stephanie were sex workers. After hearing the rumor, Stephanie confronted Sylvia, and when Sylvia confessed, Stephanie punched her in the face. But when Stephanie's boyfriend, Coy Hubbard, heard about the rumor, he brutally attacked Sylvia, slapping her and banging her head against the wall. When Gertrude found out, she viciously beat Sylvia with the paddle.

After this, Gertrude invited Coy and his fellow classmates to the house to verbally and physically assault Sylvia on a regular basis. Sylvia was beaten, burned, raped, starved, and forced to endure other humiliating and horrifying acts. Gertrude invited a neighborhood boy, Richard "Ricky" Hobbs, and his sister over and allowed them to carve the phrase "I'm a prostitute and I'm proud of it" into Sylvia's abdomen with a hot needle.

Sylvia, beaten badly for so long, was unable to use the bathroom on her own. She would often wet her bed, which Gertrude decided made her unfit to live among the other children. Gertrude locked Sylvia in the basement with no food, water, or access to a bathroom. She was kept naked and tied to the stair railing with her feet barely touching the ground.

One day, Sylvia and Jenny's older sister, Diana, tried to visit them at Gertrude's house, but Gertrude turned her away at the door. Two weeks later, Diana happened to see Jenny near the house and asked about Sylvia. Jenny nervously replied, "I can't tell you, or I'll get in trouble." The following day, Gertrude forced Sylvia to write a letter claiming that she had run away and was assaulted by several local boys— setting the boys up to take blame for her horrific abuse. However, Gertrude and John Jr. had actual plans to take Sylvia to a nearby woods, blindfold her, and abandon her there to die. Sylvia overheard them, and desperate to save herself, she tried to escape the basement. Unfortunately, her fragile, tortured body was too weak to make it far. When Gertrude caught her, she was enraged. She asked for Coy's help, and together they mercilessly beat Sylvia with a metal rod, striking her with such force that they bent the rod. Sylvia lost consciousness and Gertrude dragged her battered body back into the basement.

Sylvia tragically died on October 25, 1965, from a brain hemorrhage, shock, and severe malnutrition. When Stephanie noticed that Sylvia had stopped breathing, she attempted to perform mouth-to-mouth resuscitation. Gertrude, in complete denial, yelled at the children, claiming that Sylvia was faking her death. Gertrude grabbed a book and began striking Sylvia's lifeless body, screaming, "FAKER! FAKER!"

When the reality of Sylvia's death eventually set in, Gertrude instructed Ricky Hobbs to call the police from a nearby pay phone. When officers arrived, Gertrude led them to Sylvia's thin, bruised, and lifeless body in the basement. She handed over the letter she forced Sylvia to write. Jenny Likens, terrified of Gertrude, agreed with the false story. But as soon as she got close enough to one of the officers, she whispered, "Get me out of here, and I'll tell you everything."

After hearing Jenny's account, the police arrested Gertrude, Paula, Stephanie, and John Jr. Baniszewski, Coy Hubbard, and Ricky Hobbs for the murder of Sylvia. Other neighborhood children who participated in Sylvia's torture were also taken into custody, facing charges of injury to a person, many shifting the blame to Gertrude, claiming she had pressured them into joining the abuse.

Gertrude pleaded not guilty by reason of insanity, but she was ultimately convicted of first-degree murder and sentenced to life in prison. She was released on parole in 1985 for good behavior, a decision that outraged many. Jenny Likens, along with a large group of protesters, gathered outside the prison to condemn Gertrude's release, but their voices couldn't overturn the decision. Gertrude walked free. Stephanie, Paula, John Jr., Richard Hobbs, and Coy Hubbard were all sentenced to either life or several years in prison but also were released on parole.

Lester and Betty Likens were shattered by the systematic torture, starvation, and horrific death of their daughter Sylvia. Lester later admitted that, had he taken the time to look more closely at the

Baniszewski home before leaving his daughters there, he never would have gone through with the arrangement. The house was filthy and overcrowded, and the conditions were wholly unfit for even one child—let alone seven. Lester and Betty would carry the weight of that decision for the rest of their lives, tormented by guilt and regret. When Betty passed away in May 1998, her family discovered a small suitcase she had kept close—a "suitcase of sorrow," filled with photos of Sylvia and countless sympathy letters, a heartbreaking symbol of the grief she never let go.

THE GIRL ON THE COUCH

SLAUGHTER, LOUISIANA

2022

Lacey Fletcher was born to Sheila and Clay Fletcher on November 25, 1985, in Slaughter, Louisiana. From a young age, Lacey was diagnosed with autism spectrum disorder and social anxiety. When Lacey entered high school, classmates relentlessly bullied her, and it grew so unbearable that Lacey's parents decided to homeschool her. But rather than embracing this opportunity to support their daughter, they often complained, openly expressing their disdain for the hard work that parenting required.

Around twenty-four years old, Lacey's cognitive and physical health had drastically declined. She was confined to the living room couch, completely dependent on her parents. Instead of offering in-home or medical care, Sheila and Clay left Lacey couch-bound, surrounded by towels to catch her urine and feces. While the rest of their home was meticulously clean, the couch was completely ignored.

Sheila and Clay carried on with their lives as if nothing was wrong. They cooked, cleaned, and relaxed while their daughter was literally wasting away before their eyes. Even worse, Sheila and Clay would often leave for vacations, abandoning Lacey for days at a time. She was left to starve and sit in her own waste, completely helpless. As time passed, her clothes no longer fit her emaciated body. Her hair became completely matted. Her entire body was caked in filth. She developed bedsores across her backside so severe they were bone-deep. The couch had become Lacey's prison. For twelve agonizing years, she remained in the same position, enduring unimaginable pain and neglect, all at the hands of the very people who should protect her: her parents.

Incredibly, Sheila and Clay's neglect went unnoticed. Their neighbor Robert Blades recalled seeing Lacey exercising around the neighborhood, and after noticing her absence, he asked Clay about her, assuming she had moved away. Clay casually replied that Lacey was fine and still living at home. "I just took him on his word," Robert later said. Jess Easley, a close family friend of twenty-five years who attended weekly gatherings at the Fletchers' home, said he didn't even know they had a daughter.

By the time Lacey turned thirty-six, her body had succumbed to severe bone infections that led to sepsis—the ultimate cause of her death. On January 3, 2022, Sheila called 911, claiming she had found her daughter dead on the couch. However, it was later determined that Lacey had actually been dead for one to two days before the Fletchers decided to notify authorities.

When police arrived, they were met with a scene of pure horror. Lacey's half-naked, emaciated body, weighing just ninety-six pounds, was found fused to the couch. Maggots had infested her body and were found crawling across her corpse, feeding on her decaying flesh. Feces covered nearly every inch of her body—including her face. Ewell Bickham, the coroner who examined Lacey's body, was horrified by what he saw. Accustomed to working with the dead, he described the scene as "sickening" and said, "I couldn't eat for a week, and I cried for a week."

During questioning, Sheila and Clay's excuses were as disturbing as their actions. They claimed Lacey was "possibly" autistic and hadn't seen a therapist since her twenties, insisting she was "sound of mind" at the time of her death—a claim so detached from reality it bordered on delusion. They also claimed she stopped eating voluntarily. Sheila asserted Lacey had an intense fear of leaving the couch and refused to cooperate with them, trying to shift the blame onto their daughter. They also stood firm in their belief that Lacey died on January 3, the day they called the police.

In May 2022, four months after Lacey's horrific death, Sheila and Clay Fletcher, both sixty-six years old, were finally arrested and charged with second-degree murder. The charges initially brought a sense of hope that justice might be served for the unimaginable suffering Lacey endured. However, this hope was short-lived. The charges were reduced to manslaughter after the couple agreed to plead guilty in exchange for a lighter sentence. During their court proceedings, Sheila and Clay stated, "We loved our daughter to death"—the irony of their words was not lost on anyone. For many, this statement was nothing more than a hollow attempt to appear remorseful, a desperate ploy to gain sympathy from the court and the public.

On March 20, 2024, Sheila and Clay were sentenced to forty years in prison with twenty years suspended (meaning only twenty years are required to be served), followed by five years of supervised probation—a punishment that the public felt was woefully inadequate for the severity of their crimes.

Lacey Fletcher endured unimaginable suffering. She was abandoned, starved, and left to slowly waste away until her eventual death. Her story reminds us that evil doesn't always come in the form of strangers—it can come from the very people who are supposed to love and protect us.

CPL593H

THE PROFESSOR'S SON

FARMINGDALE, NEW YORK
2014

Patricia Ward, a sixty-six-year-old professor from Long Island, dedicated over three decades of her life to shaping young minds, earning her admiration across the Farmingdale State College's Long Island Educational Opportunity Center. Patricia was known as an innovative language arts teacher, who was deeply committed to supporting nontraditional adult and high school students, preparing them for college and beyond. To many, she was a mentor and anchor, widely admired for her kindness and warmth. Her students respected her, and her colleagues loved her.

Outside of work, Patricia lived with her thirty-five-year-old son, Derek Ward. To outsiders, they seemed like an ordinary mother-son duo. Neighbors often saw them coming and going peacefully. There were no signs of dysfunction—no arguments heard through the walls, no domestic violence complaints filed. But under the surface, Derek was struggling. For over a decade, he battled severe mental health issues. Derek also had a criminal history. He had faced charges related to drugs and weapons, and in 2014, he was unemployed and had recently completed probation. Despite his troubled past, Derek was not known to be violent. Patricia did everything she could to support her son—booking his appointments, helping him manage his prescriptions, and doing her best to keep him grounded. She was his safety net and his only advocate. But after the death of his grandfather in August 2013, his mental health significantly deteriorated.

On the night of October 28 around 7:00 p.m., neighbors glanced out their windows and saw Derek dragging a lifeless body into the street. It was Patricia's body, and in a deeply disturbing act, he kicked her severed head down the road. At first, witnesses hoped it was a Halloween stunt—some sort of macabre prank with props. But as they stepped closer, the horror became undeniable. Patricia's decapitated body lay in the middle of the road, clothed only in underwear, her head lying nearly twenty feet away.

Authorities were called immediately. Inside Patricia and Derek's home, blood was smeared across the floors and walls. A bloody kitchen knife was found near a massive pool of blood. Police determined that Derek had stabbed Patricia multiple times, breaking her ribs, then decapitated her with unnerving precision. After the murder, he reportedly sat in the blood-covered room for several minutes, perhaps in a state of shock or detachment, before dragging her mutilated body down the stairs and into the street.

After brutally murdering his mother, Derek walked aimlessly for about a mile from their Farmingdale apartment. Just before 8:00 p.m., Derek hurled himself onto the Long Island Rail Road tracks, where he was struck and killed instantly. Authorities who arrived at the scene would later connect the dots—linking Patricia's mutilated body to her son's lifeless body they found on the tracks.

In the days following, the public searched for answers. Why would Derek turn on the one person who stood by him through everything? Patricia was more than just a mother to Derek. She was also his advocate and his last remaining anchor to stability.

The community was devastated. Students mourned the loss of their beloved professor. Faculty members who had worked with Patricia for years struggled to come to terms with the cruelty of her end. Friends and neighbors were left stunned. Candlelight vigils were held in her memory.

During the investigation, it was discovered that Patricia had scheduled a psychiatric appointment for Derek—just two days following her murder. He had been going without any treatments, and four days prior to the incident, Derek had run out of his prescribed medication. She was doing everything in her power to help and protect her son. Patricia had also recently confided to her brother that Derek's behavior was becoming alarmingly erratic. He had been hearing voices, especially after the death of his grandfather—a loss that seemed to trigger the final collapse of his mental stability. People close to the family now believe that this was the moment Derek's descent into illness fully took hold. But no one could have predicted just how dark that descent would become.

THE "POSSESSION" OF MICHAEL TAYLOR

OSSETT, WEST YORKSHIRE, ENGLAND
1974

In 1974, thirty-one-year-old Michael Taylor lived in the small town of Ossett, West Yorkshire, England, with his wife, Christine, their five children, and the family dog. The Taylors appeared to be the ideal family—cheerful, loving, and well-mannered. But Michael battled with bouts of depression that stemmed from a serious back injury he'd suffered a few years prior, which left him in constant pain and struggling to secure steady employment.

At the time, Ossett was a deeply religious community, with most of its population attending church regularly. However, the Taylors were an exception; they rarely, if ever, participated in church services. Concerned for her friend Michael, Barbara Wardman suggested that he might benefit from spiritual healing. She introduced him to a local group called the Christian Fellowship Group, led by twenty-one-year-old pastor Marie Robinson. Although Michael had never been religious, he started attending the group's meetings and quickly became an active member. The teachings resonated with him, and before long, he seemed captivated by the charismatic young pastor, Marie.

Michael's involvement deepened as he spent more and more time with Marie. Their bond grew stronger, and they started conducting private rituals together. These sessions often involved staying awake all night, making the sign of the cross at each other to ward off the evil energy of the full moon. As time went on, it became evident to the group that Michael and Marie were deeply involved.

Micheal's infatuation with Marie started to spill over into his personal life, drastically altering his behavior. At home, he became distant from his family, spending far less time with them. When he was home, he was irritable, short-tempered, and seemed perpetually agitated—a stark contrast to the caring and devoted family man he had once been. Friends and family grew increasingly concerned, convinced the church group was a harmful influence on Michael. And eventually, his wife, Christine, noticed what others had already begun to suspect: Michael's feelings for Marie weren't just spiritual—they were romantic.

During a group meeting Christine was also attending, she decided she could no longer remain silent. In front of the other members, she confronted Michael, accusing him of being unfaithful and pointing out the inappropriate nature of his relationship with Marie. Her public accusation sent shock waves through the group, and Michael's already unstable behavior took an even darker turn. He claimed he felt an overwhelming and sinister presence consuming him, and this culminated in a sudden outburst of uncontrollable rage—but surprisingly, it wasn't directed at his wife, Christine. Instead, Michael turned on Marie, verbally attacking her before escalating to physical aggression. The situation became so volatile that multiple members of the group had to intervene and restrain him, fearing he might seriously harm himself or others.

Marie later described the encounter, saying, "I suddenly glanced at Mike, and his whole features changed. He looked almost bestial. He kept staring at me with a wild, terrifying look in his eyes. I started screaming at him out of sheer fear." Michael would later claim he had no recollection of this violent episode, as though it had been erased from his memory.

The day after Micheal's outburst, the group forgave him. But while they tried very hard to move past the ordeal, they couldn't shake the memory of his blowup and began to keep a closer watch on him.

Michael's behavior, however, only deteriorated further. The humiliation of being publicly accused by his wife, coupled with the rejection by Marie, seemed to unravel him completely. The once kind and composed family man began slipping deeper into a state of mental instability. Michael's erratic and alarming behavior became so concerning that local ministers took notice and decided to step in. They suspected that Michael was under the influence of demonic forces and determined that an exorcism was not only necessary but urgent.

On October 5th, 1974, Michael and Christine arrived at the church to free Michael from his demons. As the ritual began, Michael's body convulsed violently, and his behavior turned animalistic. He started scratching, spitting, and biting at those around him, forcing the priests to tie him down to the floor to prevent further harm. The exorcism continued for eight grueling hours, lasting until the early hours of the next morning. During the ritual, Michael was subjected to extreme measures. Crosses were shoved into his mouth, and he was repeatedly drenched in holy water. The priests claimed Michael was harboring forty demons within him, and after hours of relentless effort, they believed they had exorcised all but three. These remaining demons, they said, were associated with murder, violence, and insanity.

Exhausted, the priests decided to pause the exorcism and planned to resume once they had rested. Michael and Christine were sent home to recuperate.

At approximately 9:45 a.m. that same morning, barely two hours after leaving the church, police officer Ian Walker was patrolling the Taylors' neighborhood when he turned a corner and was met with a deeply unsettling sight— a naked man, covered head to toe in blood, stumbling aimlessly down the street. As Officer Walker cautiously approached, the man collapsed to the ground, curling into a fetal position and screaming, "IT'S THE BLOOD OF SATAN!" The commotion quickly drew a crowd. Friends and neighbors immediately recognized the man—it was Michael Taylor. An ambulance was called, and Michael was taken to the hospital, the entire time repeatedly screaming "It's the blood of Satan!"

One of the witnesses confirmed Michael's identity with the police and provided them with his address; Officer Walker then immediately headed to the house. As he pulled up to the Taylor residence, he saw another patrol car already parked outside. Earlier, neighbors had called the police after hearing disturbing noises coming from the house. When Officer Walker approached the entrance, he was met by a visibly shaken officer who was bent over, vomiting on the sidewalk. The officer turned to Walker, his face pale, and said, "You don't want to go in there, son. I've seen some things, but nothing like this. It's the wife... He's ripped her apart. It's a right mess in there. There's not much left of her." Despite the warning, Officer Walker braced himself and entered the home. The front room was unrecognizable. Blood covered every surface, and pieces of human flesh and brain matter were scattered across the room. In the middle of the living room lay Christine Taylor's mutilated body, barely recognizable, alongside the mangled remains of the family dog.

That morning, shortly after returning home from the exorcism, Michael descended into a horrifying and unthinkable frenzy. In a deranged attack, he turned on Christine, stripping himself naked and violently assaulting her. Overcome with rage, he strangled her and began tearing at her face with his bare hands. He gouged out her eyes, ripped out her tongue, and continued to mutilate her until her face was stripped down to the bone. The brutality left Christine completely unrecognizable. Michael's rampage didn't stop there. He turned his attention to the family dog, savagely tearing it apart limb by limb. He ripped its legs from their sockets and plucked its hair, teeth, and eyes from its skull. With the house drenched in blood, Michael stumbled outside, screaming incoherently, where Officer Walker spotted him from his patrol car.

Michael was immediately arrested at the hospital. He claimed to have no memory of the horrific events, repeatedly expressing how deeply he loved his wife and that he didn't comprehend what had happened. Despite his declarations of love, he was charged with her murder.

Michael's trial began in March 1975, where he maintained no recollection of the attack and that he had been under the influence of evil supernatural forces. The prosecution argued that the intense exorcism had pushed an already mentally unstable man to the brink, triggering the violent episode. In the end, the jury found Michael Taylor not guilty of Christine's murder by reason of insanity. As a result, he was sentenced to four years in custody: two years in Broadmoor Hospital and another two years at Bradford Royal Infirmary before being released back into society.

Over the years, the Michael Taylor case has sparked intense debate and divided opinions. Many have argued that the church should bear some accountability for Christine's tragic death, believing the exorcism distorted Michael's perception and pushed him to the brink. Others view Michael as a dangerous murderer who committed an unspeakable act and received an unduly light sentence for such a violent crime. So the question remains: Was it an outside force that took over Michael—or did his evil always lie within?

THE PORSCHE GIRL

ORANGE COUNTY, CALIFORNIA
2006

Nikki Catsouras was a shy, unassuming girl from Orange County, California. She was known as kind, energetic, and someone who left a lasting impression on everyone she met. Sadly, at just eight years old, doctors discovered a tumor in Nikki's brain, and although the tumor was benign, they recommended radiation therapy. Specialists warned her parents, Christos and Lesli, that the treatment might one day affect Nikki's ability to make sound judgments or control her impulses. As Nikki grew older, their worst fears began to manifest. Around 2005, when she was about seventeen years old, Nikki started experimenting with cocaine. One overdose left her hospitalized in a state of psychosis, a moment that rattled her parents to their cores. They blamed the radiation's aftereffects, clinging to the hope that they could guide her back to safety.

On October 30, 2006, Nikki used cocaine again. Her parents, alarmed by her deteriorating state, planned to admit her to a hospital but instead decided to schedule a psychiatric evaluation for the following day: Halloween. On Halloween day, the family shared lunch together, and Christos left for work shortly after. When Christos said goodbye, Nikki smiled at him from the couch—the day seemed ordinary. However, about ten minutes after Christos left, Lesli noticed her husband's prized Porsche 911 peel out of the driveway with Nikki behind the wheel. Panicked, she called Christos. He was stunned. Nikki knew the car was off-limits. Christos dialed 911, desperate for help. He was told to hold. When the dispatcher returned to the line, they informed him Nikki had been in an accident.

Nikki had been driving at over one hundred miles per hour when she attempted to switch lanes, clipping another car. On impact, she lost control of the Porsche, and the car was hurled over the highway median into oncoming traffic, eventually colliding with an unmanned concrete toll booth. Police arrived minutes later to find the Porsche crumpled beyond recognition. Nikki's body was still strapped into the driver's seat, but her head had been severed in the crash and split in half.

The scene was so horrific that the coroner refused to let Christos and Lesli identify their daughter's body. But tragically, they weren't spared from seeing her death. The photos from the crash were posted online, spreading rapidly through email chains, forums, MySpace pages, and hundreds of websites, dubbing her "The Porsche Girl." People offered their sympathy, but also their opinions—both good and bad. The Catsouras family soon found their inboxes flooded with the graphic images of their daughter's accident, as well as cruel messages and texts.

The situation quickly became unbearable for the Catsouras family, forcing them to take drastic measures to protect themselves. They stopped checking their emails entirely. In a desperate bid to shield their family, Christos and Lesli banned their three other daughters from using the internet. Sadly, their precautions didn't stop the torment. Nikki's sister Danielle became a direct target of the harassment. Classmates continually tried to show her the images, threatening to tape them to her locker for everyone to see. The emotional toll was devastating, and the family had no choice but to pull Danielle from school. The Catsouras family was trapped in a nightmare they couldn't wake up from.

Frustrated and desperate, the Catsouras family started looking into how the photos of Nikki's tragic accident had even made their way to the public. They soon discovered that the photos had been leaked by the California Highway Patrol. Their attorney learned that an officer had initially emailed the images to a dispatcher, who then shared them outside the department. From there, they continued to spread. The investigation identified two responsible officers. The California

Highway Patrol issued a public apology, but the damage had already been done.

One officer claimed that he had only sent the images to his personal email account so he could view them later. The other officer, however, admitted to forwarding the images of Nikki to at least four other people. The first officer was suspended without pay for twenty-five days, a punishment many believed was a slap on the wrist. The second officer, on the other hand, quit the patrol shortly after the scandal broke, though his lawyer claimed it was for unrelated reasons. For the Catsouras family, these outcomes felt far too lenient for the emotional trauma they had caused.

The Catsouras family fought tirelessly to erase the photos, contacting websites one by one in a desperate attempt to take them down. They employed advanced coding techniques to obscure the images from search engines and issued countless cease-and-desist orders, but their efforts seemed futile. Each time they managed to get the photos removed from one platform, they would reappear on another.

The Catsouras family, unhappy with how the leak was handled, decided to fight back. They filed a lawsuit against the California Highway Patrol, accusing the organization of privacy invasion, gross negligence, and inflicting unimaginable emotional distress. The legal battle was devastatingly grueling, compounding their grief, forcing them to relive the loss of their daughter and the distress that followed. After years of persistence, they finally reached a settlement of $2.37 million. For the family, the settlement wasn't a victory—it was a mere acknowledgment of a failure of trust by those who were supposed to protect them during their darkest hours.

THE EVIL SISTER

SÃO ROQUE, BRAZIL

2019

Karina Roque was a young woman living with her family in the quiet town of São Roque, Brazil. She was always described as kind, soft-spoken, and deeply loving toward her family. She had a five-year-old brother, Maycon, whom she adored and took pride in caring for. The two were often seen playing together in their yard or walking hand in hand with their mother.

On the afternoon of April 4, 2019, Karina's mother left for a shopping trip to a local store, leaving Karina in charge of watching Maycon. At eighteen years old, Karina had taken care of Maycon countless times before. About an hour later, when Karina's mother returned home, she approached the front door and immediately sensed something was off. The door wouldn't open. It was locked from the inside, and no amount of pushing or twisting would budge it. This was highly unusual. The family never locked the door when they were home, especially with children inside. Growing concerned, Karina's mother called out for Karina and Maycon, hoping to hear the familiar sound of little feet running to greet her. Instead, she heard Karina's voice—distant, flat, and emotionless. "Karina," her mother said, "open the door."

But Karina refused. "I'm not going to open it," she answered coldly.

Confusion quickly turned to panic. Her mother begged her, asking if Maycon was okay, but Karina gave no further explanation. Concerned about what was happening inside, Karina's mother contacted Karina's uncle and other nearby family members, frantically urging them to come to the house; they arrived within minutes. One by one, they pleaded with her through the door, asking her to let them in. But Karina wouldn't respond—or if she did, her words made no sense. Something felt terribly wrong. The family could feel it in their bones. This wasn't just teenage defiance. With no other option—and the rising fear that five-year-old Maycon might be in danger—Karina's uncle stepped back and began forcefully kicking at the door. Finally, with a loud crack, the door gave way and flew off its hinges.

Karina's mother collapsed the moment she saw the scene inside. Karina had brutally murdered Maycon—the brother she once protected and cared for. His small body lay lifeless, mutilated, and partially decapitated, surrounded by a circle of black candles. Blood stained the floor and walls. The family, frozen in disbelief, could barely process what they were seeing. While they were taking it all in, Karina erupted in a fit of violence and started attacking her uncle—grabbing and hurling anything and everything at him, even the furniture. Her strength was wild and unpredictable. Suddenly, she tried to bolt from the house, desperate to escape whatever madness had consumed her. Multiple family members rushed to stop her, finally wrestling her to the ground. The family dog lunged at Karina to help restrain her, too. In response, Karina bit the dog in a feral, animalistic way—her behavior almost demonic, completely detached from reality.

The family immediately called the police. Once they arrived and started examining the scene, they realized this wasn't like anything they had witnessed before. Parts of Maycon's body were missing, revealing the unthinkable: Karina had consumed pieces of her brother's flesh. The most disturbing discovery—she had mutilated his genitals and eaten them.

Karina was arrested at the scene and taken into custody. In the days that followed, she started revealing details of what had happened. She spoke to the police in a disturbingly calm and matter-of-fact way. She told investigators that after her mother left for the store, she lured Maycon into her bedroom under the pretense of playing games—something he was always excited to do. Trusting and innocent, he followed her without hesitation. Once he entered her bedroom, she attacked. Karina suffocated Maycon with a pillow, holding it down until he stopped moving. When she was sure he was unconscious, she retrieved a knife and attempted to decapitate him—but quickly discovered it wasn't as easy as she had imagined. She managed to only partially sever his neck. She then inserted the knife into both of his eyes. She burned the bottoms of his feet with a lighter. Then she mutilated his genitals and consumed them.

An autopsy would later confirm that Maycon was already dead when Karina began mutilating his body. The surrounding black candles, the placement of the body, and the ritualistic nature of the crime led authorities to suspect that the killing may have been a form of satanic or occult sacrifice.

Karina was eventually transferred to a women's prison in São Paulo. Due to the limited coverage and lack of transparency surrounding this case, little is known about her sentencing. It's been reported, but not confirmed, that she received a 112-year sentence and that she remains in solitary confinement to this day due to the extreme nature of her crime and the threat she may pose to other inmates.

While the case and its aftermath remain obscure and seemingly forgotten, Maycon must be remembered—his life ended too soon, by the sister he loved and trusted.

THE TWISTED TEEN TORMENTORS

NEW ALBANY, INDIANA
1992

Shanda Sharer was a bright light trying to find her place in the world. Living in Indiana and attending Hazelwood Middle School, Shanda was known for her bubbly personality, her friendliness, and her love of school dances. She made friends easily and had a close bond with her family, especially her mother, who was very protective of her.

In October 1991, Shanda, twelve years old at the time, happily attended her school dance and ended up meeting fourteen-year-old Amanda Heavrin. From that night, the two girls quickly became close friends and, over time, developed a romantic relationship—a relationship considered taboo in their small town at the time. Shanda would soon find out that Amanda had previously been in a relationship with sixteen-year-old Melinda Loveless, who didn't take kindly to being replaced and was enraged by Amanda's newfound connection. Melinda's jealousy quickly turned into hostility. At a later school dance, Melinda confronted the couple, publicly threatening Shanda and vowing to "get even." In the weeks that followed, she began talking to friends about hurting—or even killing—Shanda. Concerned for her daughter's safety, Shanda's mother made the difficult decision to transfer her to a different school.

Melinda's obsession, rage, and jealousy didn't go away. If anything, it intensified. Melinda decided to turn her threats into reality. She devised a plan and enlisted three other teenage girls to help her carry it out—seventeen-year-old Laurie Tackett, fifteen-year-old Hope Rippey, and fifteen-year-old Toni Lawrence. Easily swayed by Melinda's manipulations, they formed a twisted alliance, and on the night of January 10, 1992, they put their plan into motion, not everyone knowing how the night would end.

The girls drove to New Albany, Indiana, where Shanda was spending the weekend with her father. They concocted a lie to lure her out of the house: They told Shanda that Amanda wanted to see her and asked her to come along for a late-night meetup. Shanda, still holding on to her feelings for Amanda, was excited and agreed, asking them to come back after her father had gone to sleep. When they returned, Shanda snuck out of the house and into the car, ready to see Amanda. Melinda was in the back seat of the car, hidden under a blanket and clutching a knife.

Once they drove off, Melinda threw off the blanket and pressed the knife to Shanda's throat. Melinda trembled with rage as she demanded Shanda confess to "stealing" Amanda from her. Shanda immediately started crying, her body shaking with terror as she tried to stammer out a response, but her words were meaningless to Melinda. Growing angry, Melinda convinced Laurie, Toni, and Hope to take Shanda to a remote location where no one would hear her screams. They drove to a secluded trash dump in the woods near Madison, Indiana. Melinda and Laurie dragged Shanda from the car, stripping her naked in the freezing January air. They rained blows upon her body before Laurie drove her knee into Shanda's face, causing blood to gush from her nose and mouth. Meanwhile, Toni and Hope remained in the car, too frightened to intervene but complicit in their silence.

After beating her body, Melinda took out the knife and pressed it to Shanda's throat again. When the dull blade failed to cut deeply enough, she stabbed her in the chest. Then they wrapped a rope around Shanda's neck and choked her until her body went limp. Convinced they had killed her; the girls tossed Shanda's body into the trunk of the car and drove to Laurie's house. As they casually drank sodas and tried to wash away any evidence of their crime, they heard a sound from outside. It was Shanda in the trunk, trying to scream. She was still alive.

Laurie opened the trunk and started repeatedly stabbing Shanda while Melinda assaulted her with a tire iron. The girls then drove through the night with Shanda's barely conscious body still trapped in the trunk, stopping at a gas station in the early morning hours. They purchased a two-liter Pepsi bottle, poured out the soda, and filled it with gasoline.

Once they arrived at a remote field, the girls dragged Shanda out of the trunk and let her body drop to the frozen ground. Shanda managed one last word—"Mommy"—before the girls wrapped her in a blanket and poured gasoline over her body. The match ignited with a hiss, and Shanda's body was instantly engulfed in flames. As she writhed in agony, Melinda poured more gasoline, ensuring the fire consumed Shanda completely. Shanda's movements ceased, and the girls knew she was dead. They drove off, leaving her remains. Immediately after, the four girls drove to McDonald's for breakfast. They laughed and joked together, at one point even comparing the sausage they were eating to Shanda's charred body.

Later that same morning, two hunters came across Shanda's body. At first, they weren't even sure what they were looking at, but it quickly became clear they had stumbled upon something horrific, and they immediately called the authorities.

Once the police were notified, it didn't take long for the girls to share their secret. That evening, guilt eating away at them, Toni and Hope went to the Jefferson County Police Department with their parents and confessed. They told detectives the full story in graphic detail, including the locations, the timeline, and exactly what each girl had done. Meanwhile, Melinda and Laurie almost immediately told Amanda and another friend, Crystal, who both didn't believe the girls until they saw the bloodied trunk. By the next day, all four girls—Melinda Loveless, Laurie Tackett, Toni Lawrence, and Hope Rippey—were in police custody.

Due to the extreme brutality of the crime, all four teens were tried as adults. Toni Lawrence, the youngest, was sentenced to twenty years. She was released in 2000. Hope Rippey was originally sentenced to fifty years, which was later reduced to thirty-five years on appeal. Despite her participation in the planning and the final act of setting Shanda on fire, she was released in 2006. Laurie Tackett and Melinda Loveless—the two most directly involved—each received sixty-year sentences. However, neither served their full term. Laurie was released in 2018 after just over twenty-five years. Melinda followed a year later, released in 2019 after serving twenty-six years.

Shanda's parents were utterly devastated, especially her mother, Jacque Vaught. During the trial, Jacque gave a profound speech while photographs from Shanda's life flashed behind her. She shared her most cherished memories of her daughter, leaving the courtroom emotional in a stunned silence. Directing her words at her daughter's killer, she said, "Melinda has cheated me out of being with my daughter during this life. It is my wish for you that you live your life with the memories of her screams and the sight of her burned and mutilated body." Her voice steady but filled with grief, Jacque continued, "I'm not sure who you love most in life, Melinda, whether it be your mother or your father, but I want you to imagine them in the trunk of that car. I want you to imagine the person you love the most begging and screaming for their life." It was a moment of raw, unfiltered anguish—a mother speaking from a place of unimaginable pain, hoping that her words would echo in Melinda's conscience for the rest of her life.

THE MAN ON THE BUS

WINNIPEG, MANITOBA, CANADA
2008

Tim McLean was widely regarded as a kindhearted, outgoing, and generous person. He worked seasonally as a carnival worker, which fit his friendly nature. On July 30, 2008, after working as part of a traveling fair in Edmonton, he boarded a Greyhound Canada bus to his hometown of Winnipeg, Manitoba. He was looking forward to reuniting with his pregnant girlfriend, who was eagerly awaiting his return so they could start the next chapter of their lives together. Tim found a seat toward the back of the bus, slipped on his headphones, and began listening to music.

Around 6:00 p.m., after the bus stopped in Erickson, forty-year-old Vince Li boarded. From the moment he stepped on, passengers noticed he seemed restless and disoriented, staring blankly and occasionally muttering to himself. Li initially took a seat near the front of the bus, but after a brief rest stop in Brandon, he quietly moved toward the back, eventually settling in next to Tim, who had dozed off with his head resting against the window.

Without any warning or provocation, Li pulled out a large knife and began savagely stabbing Tim in the neck and chest, launching into a frenzied, relentless attack. Passengers screamed and rushed to alert the driver, who immediately pulled over and evacuated the bus. Passengers ran for their lives, and only a young Army veteran and a truck driver were brave enough to intervene. However, Li wildly waved the knife at anyone who tried to get close, forcing them to back away.

Despite the chaos, Vince Li continued his brutal assault on Tim's lifeless body. Then, to every passenger's horror, he decapitated Tim and held his severed head up to the bus window like a trophy. The screams from the crowd were gut-wrenching—some fainted, others vomited. But Li continued to mutilate Tim's body, removing organs and eating parts of his flesh in plain view.

Police were immediately called, and once they knew the severity of the situation—including the beheading—officers rushed to the scene in full force. Upon arrival, police found Vince Li still on board the bus, pacing back and forth calmly, emotionless, with Tim McLean's severed head in his hand. For the next five hours, law enforcement attempted to defuse the standoff. Negotiators spoke through loudspeakers while a perimeter was set to keep the growing crowd at a safe distance. Vince occasionally walked back and forth in the aisle, muttering to himself and holding pieces of Tim's dismembered body. The tension continued to escalate. Then, just after midnight, Vince tried to escape by smashing one of the bus windows. It was then that officers deployed a Taser, hitting him twice and enabling them to handcuff him and place him in the back of a police cruiser.

Once Vince was detained, police boarded the bus and were met with pure carnage. Blood was splattered everywhere, and Tim McLean's remains were scattered throughout the vehicle. While parts of Tim's body were retrieved from the bus and placed in evidence bags, his heart and both of his eyes were completely missing. Investigators eventually concluded that Vince had consumed them. When Li was finally searched, they found Tim's ear, nose, and tongue stuffed inside his pocket.

In March 2009, after a psychiatric evaluation and trial, Vince Li was found not criminally responsible for Tim's murder due to severe mental illness, later diagnosed as untreated schizophrenia. Instead of prison, he was sent to Selkirk Mental Health Centre, a secure psychiatric facility in Manitoba.

In 2012, Vince Li finally spoke publicly about his motive. He claimed he was hearing the voice of God, which instructed him to kill Tim in order to protect humanity from an impending alien invasion.

And not just to kill him, but to mutilate his body to ensure he couldn't "come back to life."

"The voice told me I was the third story of the Bible," he said, "that I was like the second coming of Jesus and that I was to save people from a space alien attack." Li explained that in the days leading up to the murder, he had been following the voice's instructions closely, traveling across Canada by bus as part of a divine mission. He believed he was in constant danger and carried a Buck knife for protection—the knife he used to end Tim McLean's life. He said he was unaware that he was suffering from schizophrenia at the time.

In February 2017, less than a decade after the murder, Vince Li was granted an absolute discharge. The Criminal Code Review Board concluded that he was no longer a threat to the public, no longer required psychiatric reviews, and was no longer subject to monitoring of any kind. Following his release, Vince legally changed his name to Will Lee Baker.

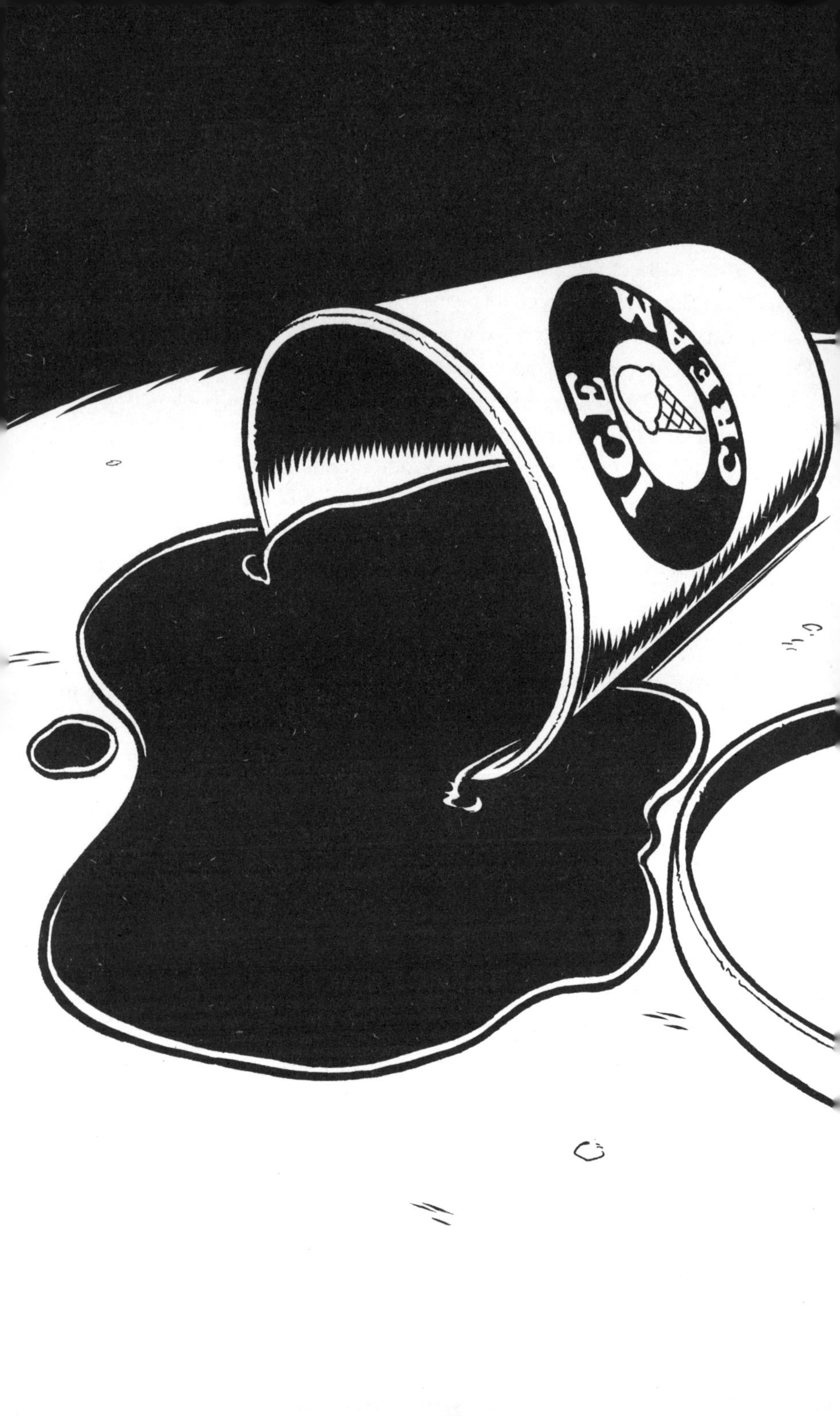
ICE CREAM

THE KILLER WHO LEFT ALL THE EVIDENCE BEHIND

TOKYO, JAPAN
2000

The Miyazawa family of four—Mikio, his wife, Yasuko, and their children Niina and Rei—lived a quiet, peaceful life in the Setagaya ward of Tokyo, Japan. Mikio worked for Interbrand, an international marketing firm. He was known by colleagues as a dedicated and diligent professional, while neighbors described him as kind and attentive. Yasuko was a loving mother and part-time teacher who was just as beloved in their community. Niina and Rei were cheerful, well-mannered, and adored by both their teachers and classmates. They lived in a modern, two-story home connected by a shared hallway with Yasuko's parents' residence, where Yasuko's mother, sister, and brother-in-law lived—symbolizing their tight familial bond.

When they first moved into the area in 1990, the neighborhood was bustling, with over two hundred families occupying the suburban enclave. However, by the end of the decade, city redevelopment initiatives pushed many families to relocate. The once-busy neighborhood had grown ominously quiet. Eventually, only four families remained, including the Miyazawas. Despite many discussions about moving out, the Miyazawas stayed put.

Then, around December 2000, a series of distressing events cast a shadow over their otherwise routine lives. Mikio, fed up with the excessive noise a group of teens was making at the skate park directly behind his house, confronted them, yelling to quiet down. Another time, for the same reason, it's believed Mikio had harsh words with members of the Bōsōzoku, a notorious and often violent Japanese biker gang. Around the same time, the family began noticing a strange vehicle repeatedly parked near their home, always unoccupied but still raising concern.

On December 30, 2000, the Miyazawa family went about their day as usual. Around 6:00 p.m., they went out shopping in preparation for the upcoming New Year's celebrations—a time typically filled with joy and family gatherings. They returned home about an hour later, likely planning to relax and welcome the new year together.

The next morning, Yasuko's mother became concerned after the family didn't pick up any of her numerous phone calls. She went next door and knocked, but there was no answer. Trusting her instincts, she used the shared hallway to enter the home—and stumbled into a nightmare. Mikio's body was found at the base of the stairs, stabbed multiple times. Upstairs, Yasuko and Niina were discovered in the bedroom, both viciously stabbed to death. In another room, young Rei was found strangled in his bed, likely killed in his sleep. The entire family had been slaughtered inside their own home—no signs of forced entry, no sounds loud enough to alert nearby residents, and no clear motive.

When police arrived at the Miyazawa residence, they were met with a crime scene unlike anything they had ever seen. It wasn't just the brutality of the murders—it was the strangeness of what was left behind. Investigators immediately identified the murder weapons: a sashimi knife—brought by the killer, purchased just one day before the crime—and one of the family's kitchen knives. The sashimi knife was used in the initial assault on Mikio and reportedly broke during the frenzied attack, suggesting an extreme level of force. The killer then switched to the kitchen knife, which was used in the murders of Yasuko and Niina.

Based on forensic analysis and the positions of the bodies, investigators pieced together a possible sequence of events. They theorized that the killer entered the home through a second-floor bathroom window that had been left unlocked—a point of entry that required significant agility and planning. Once inside, the killer is believed to have made his way to Rei's bedroom first, where the six-year-old was strangled in his sleep. Afterward, the killer encountered Mikio. A violent struggle took place between the two. Mikio was found dressed in business clothes, which implied he had been working late and had just come in or was possibly getting ready for bed. Following Mikio's murder, the killer made his way upstairs and brutally stabbed Yasuko and Niina. The excessive nature of their injuries, especially postmortem wounds, suggested personal animosity or psychotic rage.

As the investigation dove deeper, their discoveries got stranger. Instead of fleeing the scene, the killer lingered. He remained inside the home for hours. He left behind a robust trail of DNA and physical evidence throughout the house: defecating in the toilet without flushing, bleeding throughout the home on feminine products and towels, and leaving footprints and fingerprints behind—including on doorknobs, walls, food wrappers, and even the computer.

The killer's behavior after the murders bordered on surreal. He rummaged through the refrigerator and ate ice cream, he drank a cup of barley tea, and at one point, he even made himself comfortable on the living room couch and took a nap. If that wasn't strange enough, he used Mikio's home computer twice: once at 1:18 a.m., just hours after the murders, to browse the internet and attempt to purchase theater tickets, and again at 10:05 a.m. to look at websites associated with Mikio's workplace and Yasuko's school. This indicated that the killer remained in the home long after sunrise, completely unbothered by the dead family, the presence of nearby neighbors, or the possibility of being caught.

The police later collected multiple strange sightings on the night of the murder. Around 10:00 p.m., a neighbor reported hearing raised voices and what sounded like an argument coming from the Miyazawa residence. Another witness came forward saying they saw a man near the home with blood on his hands. A taxi driver later reported picking up three men near the neighborhood—one of whom had a hand wound severe enough to leave bloodstains in the vehicle. These unsettling reports, however, didn't bring police any closer to finding the killer.

Over the years, Japanese authorities have poured immense resources into solving the crime, but despite the overwhelming evidence—DNA, witness accounts, clothing, fingerprints, and the murder weapons—the Setagaya family murders remain unsolved. More than 280,000 officers and investigators have worked on the case, one of the largest criminal investigations in Japan's history.

Some believe the killer may have died, while others think he could be living freely under a new identity, possibly even outside of Japan. It's as if he vanished into thin air after committing one of the most brutal and bizarre crimes Japan has ever seen.

CHAPTER FIVE

THE UNEXPLAINED

Unsolved Mysteries and Other Strange Phenomena

THE TWINS' RETURN

HEXHAM, ENGLAND
1958

Joanna and Jacqueline Pollock, daughters of John and Florence Pollock, were vibrant, loving children—the heart and soul of the Pollock household. With three older brothers, the girls were known to be inseparable. On the morning of May 5, 1957, eleven-year-old Joanna, six-year-old Jacqueline, and their friend Anthony were walking to church along a road in Hexham, England, when a car suddenly veered onto the sidewalk and struck all three children. The driver was a local woman, later found to be under the influence of drugs and alcohol. After recently losing custody of her children, she suffered a mental breakdown. In an apparent act of despair and rage, she deliberately drove her car into the children. Joanna and Jacqueline were killed instantly, and Anthony succumbed to his injuries shortly after being rushed to the hospital.

Their three deaths sent shock waves through the community. The deaths of Joanna and Jacqueline plunged John and Florence into a deep state of grief and despair. John's devastation, however, was tinged with a strange sense of hope. A devout Catholic, John believed in life after death—but also in the possibility of reincarnation, a belief that clashed with traditional Christian teachings. Even as he mourned, he began to confide in Florence that he believed Joanna and Jacqueline would return to them in some form. His wife, however, was more skeptical and preferred to focus on healing from their unbearable loss.

A year later, Florence became pregnant. Medical scans and family history gave no indication of twins, but John was adamant—he was certain she would give birth to twin girls. Against all odds, he was right. On October 4th, 1958, Florence gave birth to identical twin daughters, Gillian and Jennifer Pollock. From the very beginning, the family couldn't help but notice odd and almost unsettling similarities between the twins and their deceased sisters.

Most notably, Jennifer had two birthmarks that mirrored Jacqueline's: one on her forehead, which was nearly identical in shape and location to Jacqueline's scar from falling onto a bucket, and another on her waist, where Jacqueline also had a distinctive birthmark. Even though Gillian had no such marks, she began to take on the older sibling role—just as Joanna had once done. As the twins grew older, their behaviors, mannerisms, and even preferences began to echo those of their late sisters. The family watched in awe and a bit of apprehension as the girls requested specific toys that had once belonged to Joanna and Jacqueline—toys that had been stored away and never shown to them.

When the twins were four years old, the family returned to Hexham for the first time since the tragedy. Though the twins had never been to the town before, they seemed to know their way around instinctively. The girls pointed out landmarks from Joanna and Jacqueline's past, including the school they had attended and a local playground. They even used phrases like, "That's where we used to play."

One day, Florence walked into a room to find her daughter Gillian cradling Jennifer's head, whispering, "The blood's coming out of your eyes... That's where the car hit you." Florence was shocked—not only by its graphic nature but also by how closely it matched the injuries sustained by Jacqueline, who had been struck in the head during the fatal car accident years earlier. Gillian, a child who should have had no knowledge of that gruesome detail, spoke as if she had seen it happen firsthand. Following this incident, the twins began to show an intense and irrational fear of cars. Whenever a vehicle passed by or even came into view, they would instinctively grab Florence's hand, their knuckles going white with fear. The sight or sound of a car seemed to trigger a deep, unexplainable panic within them. One particular event stood out to their parents: John was inside the house when he suddenly heard his daughters screaming in terror. He rushed to the room, only to find them huddled together in a corner, shaking and crying, clinging to each other like their lives depended on it. Outside, a car engine had simply started up—but to the twins, it was as though they were reliving a past trauma.

As time went on, these intense memories, inexplicable knowledge, and shared behaviors that mirrored their deceased sisters began to fade, noticeably around the time the twins turned five years old. But by then, their story had already started to gain attention. It eventually caught the eye of Dr. Ian Stevenson, a psychiatrist from the University of Virginia renowned for his extensive work in studying cases of children who remember past lives. Intrigued by the numerous parallels between the twins and their late sisters, Stevenson traveled to England and began a thorough investigation. He conducted multiple interviews with John, Florence, Gillian, and Jennifer over the course of many years. What he found deeply fascinated—and disturbed—him.

Dr. Stevenson took particular interest in Jacqueline's birthmarks, the girls' behaviors, and their knowledge of places and objects they had never encountered yet. He followed up with the twins in adulthood, keeping in touch even after their parents passed away. He believed that even though the twins no longer had new memories of their supposed past lives, their childhood recollections had been too specific, too detailed, and too emotionally charged to simply be dismissed as coincidence.

Despite their eventual memory loss of their past lives, Gillian and Jennifer never rejected their parents' belief that they were somehow the reincarnated versions of Joanna and Jacqueline. In fact, they seemed to accept it as a strange truth of their existence—something they could feel, even if they couldn't remember. They went on to live normal, healthy lives, yet the events of their early years would stay with them forever. It's a story that continues to fascinate, baffle, and intrigue, begging the question: What if we really do come back?

THE EXORCISM OF ANNELIESE MICHEL

BAVARIA, WEST GERMANY

1968

Anneliese Michel, born in 1952, grew up in a devout Roman Catholic household in Bavaria, West Germany. Her family—parents Anna and Josef, and her three younger sisters—Roswitha, Gertrud, and Barbara—attended mass twice a week and read the Bible daily. Anneliese and her sisters were raised with a strong sense of faith and encouraged to atone for their sins.

In 1968, when Anneliese was just sixteen years old, she blacked out during school, losing consciousness and waking up with no memory of the event. Her classmates described her as being in a trancelike state. A year later, she had another blackout, this time more severe. She lost control of her bladder, wetting herself, and experienced violent tremors and convulsions. During these episodes, Anneliese felt a heavy force pressing down on her. Alarmed, her family sought medical help. She was taken to a neurologist, Dr. Siegfried Lüthy, who conducted an electroencephalogram (EEG). The results were normal, but Dr. Lüthy suspected Annaliese was suffering from grand mal seizures. However, since she had experienced only two episodes at that point, he decided not to prescribe medication, leaving Anneliese without a clear diagnosis.

As Anneliese continued her treatment with Dr. Lüthy, her physical health began to deteriorate rapidly. Her tonsils became severely inflamed, requiring a tonsillectomy. Following the surgery, she developed pneumonia, which was further complicated by tuberculosis.

These mounting health issues forced her to withdraw from school, disrupting her education and isolating her even more.

By 1970, her condition had worsened to the point that she was admitted to a hospital specializing in pediatric lung diseases. But despite the specialized care, her health showed no signs of improvement. Eventually, she was transferred to a tuberculosis clinic in Bavaria for more intensive treatment. During her stay at the clinic, Anneliese distanced herself from the other children undergoing treatment. This behavior earned her the reputation of being stuck-up and antisocial.

At the clinic, Anneliese experienced her third seizure. This one struck at night, leaving her paralyzed in bed, unable to move or cry for help. She again felt a crushing weight on her body and lost control of her bladder. When the episode ended, Anneliese awoke screaming in terror. Her cries echoed through the hospital. The other children began mocking her, claiming she was possessed by the devil. When staff found her, her face was twisted into an angry expression, and her hands were contorted, with her fingertips locked tightly into her palms in a clawlike position. Only days later, Anneliese was praying the rosary when she suddenly smelled violets in the air. Her hands froze into the same clenched position as before, but a wave of euphoria also washed over her, an overwhelming sense of peace that seemed almost divine. The feeling persisted throughout the day, and Anneliese became convinced it was a sign from the Virgin Mary.

Anneliese eventually sought the help of another neurologist, Dr. Von Haller, who conducted an EEG and detected irregular brain waves. He diagnosed her with a form of epilepsy and prescribed new medication to control her seizures. However, the treatments proved ineffective. During one of these episodes, Anneliese reported seeing a menacing face—a haunting vision that would torment her for the rest of her life.

Over time, her condition stabilized, and she was discharged from the hospital, finally returning home to her family. But once she was back at home, Anneliese's personality began to change dramatically;

she often erupted in anger and blamed the church for her condition. By 1973, Anneliese believed the devil was inside her. She confided in Dr. Lüthy, who determined that she was no longer capable of making her own decisions. Her condition was now thought to be a combination of epilepsy and schizophrenia or bipolar disorder. This diagnosis marked a turning point, as her mental and emotional state declined again. Depression set in, and Anneliese began contemplating suicide. She believed the world was ending.

At the same time, she felt a profound connection to the Virgin Mary, clinging to her faith as a source of solace. But soon, her visions of devilish faces became more frequent, and whispers plagued her prayers, telling her she was damned and would rot in hell. Anneliese started tearing off her clothes and obsessively performing four hundred squats a day to the point of exhaustion. She inflicted harm upon herself, barked like a dog for two consecutive days, ate spiders, bit the head off a dead bird, and even licked her own urine from the floor. Anneliese's friends, family, and members of her community started to suspect this was something far beyond medical explanation. Whispers of demonic possession spread. Her parents, desperate for answers and a way to help their daughter, started exploring treatments outside conventional medicine, considering the possibility that she was afflicted by something supernatural.

Anneliese started seeing Father Ernst Alt, a Roman Catholic priest. He claimed he was able to distinguish between demonic possession and physical or mental illness. After spending time with Anneliese, Father Alt was convinced that her condition was beyond medical explanation and sought help from Bishop Josef Stangl. The bishop, despite knowing Anneliese's medical history, approved an exorcism. He assigned the task to a local priest, Father Arnold Renz, and insisted the exorcism be carried out in complete secrecy. The exorcism sessions consisted of chanting, scripture readings, and ritual prayers repeated for up to four hours, depending on the circumstances. Anneliese's first exorcism session took place on September 24, 1975. Over the next ten months, she endured a staggering sixty-seven sessions. At this point, her parents placed their complete faith in the exorcisms, abandoning all medical treatment. Anneliese's weight plummeted and her health rapidly declined, but she still displayed abnormal strength during her sessions.

Anneliese claimed she was inhabited by six demons: Lucifer, Cain, Judas Iscariot, Adolf Hitler, Nero, and a disgraced priest named Fleishmann. The demons were said to speak through her during the exorcisms, reinforcing her parents' and the priests' convictions. The demons allegedly fought for control over Anneliese's body, their presence marked by guttural growls and disturbing vocalizations. Audio recordings reveal unsettling exchanges during which the demons argued with each other—Judas purportedly mocking Hitler as a "big mouth who had no say in hell."

Father Renz also devised a test using five bottles filled with water—some containing tap water, others holy water. When he sprinkled Annaliese with tap water, she had no reaction. When he sprinkled her with holy water, Anneliese reportedly started howling and thrashing. During the exorcism sessions, she frequently had to be restrained. Over time, she stopped eating and drinking, claiming the demons forbade her from doing so. With her health deteriorating, she barely slept. When awake, she reportedly ran through the house, pleading with Jesus for mercy. Despite her worsening condition, the priests and her parents remained steadfast in their belief that she was possessed.

Her final exorcism session took place on June 30, 1976. By this point, Anneliese was severely emaciated, physically broken, and emotionally drained. During the session, she made a heartbreaking final request to her mother: "Mama, stay with me. I'm scared." Following this last ritual, the priests declared that all demons had been exorcised from her body.

The next day, on July 1, 1976, Anneliese was found dead—by her mother—at just twenty-three years old. While a physician first noted that her death did not appear to result from natural causes, her autopsy later revealed that Anneliese had died from advanced emaciation caused by severe dehydration and malnutrition; she weighed only about seventy pounds at the time of her death. The examination also showed fractured teeth, pneumonia, and ruptured knee ligaments—likely caused by the estimated six hundred genuflections during exorcism sessions.

After her death, Father Alt contacted the district attorney's office—defending the church's actions and explaining that the exorcisms were conducted under the conviction of demonic possession. Shockingly, he remained adamant that Anneliese was not ill and insisted he would have sought medical help if he had thought otherwise.

The trial of those who were held responsible for Anneliese Michel's death began on March 30, 1978. Her parents, Josef and Anna, and the two priests, Father Ernst Alt and Father Arnold Renz, were charged with negligent homicide. During the trial, audio recordings from the exorcisms were shared, filling the courtroom with Anneliese's growls and screams. While the defense tried to use them to validate their claim of demonic possession, the prosecution cited them as evidence of psychological distress and neglect. On April 21, 1978, all four defendants were convicted and received a six-month suspended sentence and three years of probation.

THE CHRISTMAS EVE MYSTERY

FAYETTEVILLE, WEST VIRGINIA

1945

George and Jennie Sodder were proud, hardworking Italian American parents, raising ten children in Fayetteville, West Virgina. They lived in a modest two-story home just outside of town and were well-known in the community. George, who had immigrated from Italy, ran a successful trucking business, and Jennie stayed home with the children. Life was not without its challenges—George held strong political views, especially his vocal criticism of Mussolini, which had sparked tension with some other Italian Americans in the area—but for the most part, the Sodders lived a normal life.

On Christmas Eve 1945, the Sodder family gathered in their home to celebrate the holidays. Nine of the ten children were present; their second-eldest son, Joe, was away serving in World War II. Around 10:00 p.m., George and the two oldest boys, John and George Jr., had already gone to bed. Jennie tucked in the youngest child, two-year-old Sylvia, and laid down herself soon after. The older daughter, Marion, stayed up with five of the younger siblings—Maurice, Martha, Louis, Jennie, and Betty. They were allowed to stay up late as a special holiday treat, playing with new toys Marion had brought them earlier that day from her job at a local dime store.

At around 12:30 a.m., the quiet of the night was disturbed when the phone rang. Jennie got up to answer it. On the line was an oddly cheerful woman's voice, asking for someone unfamiliar, with laughter echoing in the background. Jennie did not recognize the caller's voice, so she told the woman she had the wrong number and hung up. After, Jennie noticed that all the lights were still on and the curtains wide open—something that struck her as unusual. She turned everything off and closed the curtains before heading back to bed. But she wasn't asleep long when she was awoken again—this time by a loud thud on the roof, followed by a strange rolling sound, almost like something had landed and bounced across the shingles. Then, just before 1:00 a.m., she awoke once more—but this time to the scent of thick, choking smoke. When she bolted upright, she saw that George's office was on fire, flames quickly spreading through the house.

Panic set in immediately. Jennie and George rushed to get Sylvia and themselves out, while Marion, John, and George Jr. also managed to escape. But the five younger children—Maurice, Martha, Louis, Jennie, and Betty—were nowhere to be found. They were last seen heading upstairs to the attic to sleep, but the stairs were already completely engulfed in flames, blocking any access.

The house phone was dead, so Marion ran to a neighbor's house to call for help. Meanwhile, George tried to reach the attic window from outside. He raced to grab his ladder—which was always propped against the house—but it had mysteriously vanished. Then he tried starting both of his trucks, thinking he could drive them up to the house and climb onto the roof, but both engines failed to start, despite working the day before.

Neighbors tried calling the fire department, but at the time Fayetteville didn't have a centralized emergency service. The fire chief, F. J. Morris, had to initiate a "phone tree" system, calling in volunteers one by one. It took seven hours for the fire crew to arrive. The house had reportedly been destroyed in forty-five minutes and, by then, was just a pile of ash and rubble. The initial search of the property yielded no trace of human remains—no bones, no teeth, no physical evidence to suggest that five children had died in the fire. Authorities assumed the five missing children had perished in the fire, claiming the blaze burned so intensely it cremated their bodies completely. But Jennie didn't believe it. Determined, she consulted a crematorium worker, who explained that even after burning at 2,000 degrees Fahrenheit for over two hours, human bones do not fully disintegrate. The Sodders' home had only burned for about forty-five minutes, and it was an open-air fire, not nearly hot enough to destroy bodies. If the children had died in that blaze, some remains should have been found—but there were none.

Leading up to the fire, George experienced several ominous signs. A traveling insurance salesman, frustrated when George declined to buy a policy and upset by his anti-Mussolini views, warned him that his house would "go up in smoke" and that his children would be destroyed. George's fierce political stance had already made him an enemy in the community, and now this threat took on a horrifying new weight. Another person, looking for work, wandered around the property and remarked casually that the fuse boxes were going to "cause a fire someday," despite George having just had the house rewired and inspected.

After the fire and news of the children spread, reports and sightings started flooding in. One local claimed they saw the Sodder children peering out the back of a car, watching the fire as it consumed their home. Another witness, who worked at a tourist stop about fifty miles away, claimed that the morning after the fire, she served breakfast to a group of children matching the Sodder kids' descriptions. They were reportedly accompanied by two adults who spoke Italian, and she remembered the group acting nervous, refusing to speak openly.

George and Jennie, hearing these accounts and convinced their children hadn't burned to ashes, started to suspect their missing children had been kidnapped, perhaps as a punishment for George's political beliefs or a way to silence him. Desperate for answers, the Sodders petitioned local authorities and even wrote directly to the FBI. To their surprise, J. Edgar Hoover himself replied to George's letters, expressing sympathy but ultimately declining to get involved. Hoover stated that the case was outside federal jurisdiction unless the local police requested assistance—which they never did.

In 1952, as the years dragged on without answers, the Sodders erected a massive billboard along Route 16, just a short distance from where their home had once stood. It featured pictures of the five missing children and asked, in bold letters: "What Was Their Fate?" The billboard became a landmark in Fayetteville, drawing visitors, reporters, and conspiracy theorists alike. For decades, it stood as a painful, public plea for justice, a symbol of parents who never gave up hope.

George and Jennie dedicated the rest of their lives to chasing every possible lead. They traveled across the country, following anonymous tips, interviewing witnesses, and even hiring private detectives—some of whom mysteriously vanished or gave up without explanation. In 1969, George passed away, heartbroken, having searched for his children to the very end and never finding them. Jennie, who spent her final years dressed entirely in black for her children, died in 1989. After her death, the remaining Sodder children quietly took the billboard down. To this day, the fate of the Sodder children remains a chilling Christmas Eve mystery.

THE HINTERKAIFECK FARM

BAVARIA, GERMANY

1922

The Hinterkaifeck farmstead was home to Viktoria Gabriel, who was widowed, and her two children—Cäzilia and Josef—along with her elderly parents Andreas and Cäzilia Gruber. The farmstead was isolated in the woods, located between the Bavarian towns of Ingolstadt and Schrobenhausen. The family was known to be private, staying to themselves for the most part.

In March 1922, Andreas Gruber discovered a newspaper from Munich sitting on the property, which no one in the family had purchased. At first, Andreas assumed it was a harmless delivery error, but when he asked around, no one in the area subscribed to that unique newspaper. Shortly afterward, Andreas also noticed a set of unfamiliar footprints leading from the nearby woods toward the farm, but curiously, there were no tracks leading away. Concerned, he searched the house, particularly the attic where strange noises had been heard before. He found nothing—no signs of an intruder, no damage, and no additional clues. The family did, however, notice their house keys were missing. Concerned, Andreas told neighbors and locals about his concerns, but no one seemed overly worried.

That same month, the Gruber family welcomed a new maid, Maria Baumgartner. She was hired to replace their previous maid, who had abruptly quit a year earlier. Rumors in the nearby village were that the previous maid left when she became convinced the house was haunted, saying she heard footsteps creak through the attic at night. For months, the family struggled, but on March 31, 1922, Maria put in her first day of work, eventually settling down for the night in her bedroom.

The next day, several townspeople stopped by the Hinterkaifeck farm. They weren't alarmed when no one answered the door, considering the family's reclusive nature. But concerns grew when the family failed to attend church on Sunday—a ritual they never missed—and Viktoria's daughter, Cäzilia, missed several days of school, with no explanation provided by the family.

On April 4th, 1922, a concerned neighbor, Lorenz Schlittenbauer, accompanied by two other men, decided to visit the Hinterkaifeck farm to check on the family. They could no longer ignore their own concerns or those of the village. As the men approached the farm, they were immediately struck by the deafening silence. They decided to check the barn, where they discovered the bodies of Andreas, Cäzilia, Viktoria, and Viktoria's young daughter—buried beneath hay and debris. They had been murdered in a disturbingly violent manner, attacked with a mattock, their skulls shattered by vicious blows.

After the horrifying discovery in the barn, the men rushed into the main house, hoping that someone had survived. But inside, they found the newly hired maid Maria Baumgartner murdered in her bed. Nearby in his crib lay two-year-old Josef, the youngest member of the family, also brutally killed. The entire household had been slaughtered, without a single neighbor hearing or witnessing a thing.

The men immediately notified authorities. From the start, the case was plagued with questions and contradictions. Initially, investigators considered it a robbery. But when large sums of money were found untouched in the house, that theory quickly fell apart. In fact, nothing appeared to be stolen—at least nothing of value. What police did discover was that the killer had stayed on the farm several days after the murders, feeding the livestock, milking the cows, and even cooking meals in the kitchen. Warm embers were found in the fireplace, and fresh food had been prepared. The killer was comfortable enough to live among the dead.

As the case gained national and eventually international attention, deeper investigations into the family's past started to reveal disturbing secrets. In 1914, Andreas Gruber was convicted of incest with his daughter Viktoria, a charge that resulted in a one-year prison sentence for him, and one month for Viktoria. That same year, Viktoria's husband, Karl Gabriel, was reportedly killed in World War I. However, his body was never officially recovered, and some locals whispered that he may have faked his death or somehow survived. It has also been speculated that Josef was the product of the incestuous relationship between Viktoria and her father. Others believe Viktoria may have had a secret lover from the village. One theory even suggests that Karl was not killed during the war but instead learned of his wife's relationship with her father, returned to Hinterkaifeck, and massacred everyone in a fit of rage.

Despite over a century of speculation, investigation, and obsession, the Hinterkaifeck murders have become a symbol of the "perfect crime"—unsolved, unprovable, unattributed, and cunning in its execution. As time goes on, the truth of what happened that day may have died with its victims.

A DEADLY EXPEDITION

DUTCH NEW GUINEA (NOW PAPUA)

1961

Michael Rockefeller was born on May 18, 1938, into one of the wealthiest and most powerful families in American history. He was the youngest son of Nelson Rockefeller, future governor of New York and vice president of the United States, and the great-grandson of John D. Rockefeller, the world's first billionaire and wealthiest American of all time. Michael seemed destined to follow the path laid out before him—managing investments, rubbing shoulders with dignitaries, and upholding the family legacy of influence and wealth. But Michael was different.

Unlike his gregarious father, Michael was soft-spoken, introspective, and drawn to the world beyond boardrooms and balance sheets. After graduating from Harvard in 1960, he found himself restless, uninterested in a life of endless meetings and corporate responsibility. An adventurer at heart, he craved something more meaningful and was fascinated by culture, traditions, and community.

Much of that curiosity was sparked by his father's passion for art. Nelson had founded the Museum of Primitive Art in New York City, a collection that showcased non-Western art from African, Oceanic, and pre-Columbian civilizations. The museum's artifacts—from Nigerian carvings to Aztec sculptures—captivated Michael.

Michael joined the museum's board and began making plans to acquire and collect art firsthand, seeking to contribute something entirely his own. His interest soon turned to Dutch New Guinea, now known as Papua, an island north of Australia. Michael was particularly drawn to the Asmat people, a tribal group known for their striking woodcarvings, deep spiritual traditions, and their history of headhunting and cannibalism. Although Dutch colonial authorities had maintained a presence on the island since the 1950s, many Asmat villages remained isolated.

In 1961, Michael joined a documentary and research team on a scouting expedition to the Asmat region. The group arrived in the village of Otsjanep, one of the major Asmat settlements. While they allowed photographers to capture parts of village life, the Asmat refused to part with their sacred cultural artifacts—their intricately carved shields and bisj poles, used in ancestral rituals. When the expedition ended, Michael returned home briefly, but he was determined to go back. He was more inspired than ever to return, build a comprehensive anthropological study, and bring Asmat artwork back to the Museum of Primitive Art.

In 1961, just months after his first expedition, Michael Rockefeller returned to Dutch New Guinea—this time without a full research crew. Accompanying him was René Wassing, a Dutch anthropologist. Michael was more resolute than ever to acquire Asmat artifacts for his father's museum and deepen his personal connection to the tribe's culture. Over three weeks, they visited thirteen villages, collecting artifacts like spears, shields, drums, and several bisj poles. On November 17, 1961, the two men set out by boat, once again aiming for the village of Otsjanep, home to one of the more traditional Asmat communities.

But this time, something went terribly wrong. Rough seas caused their catamaran to capsize, flipping the vessel and leaving both Michael and René clinging to its overturned hull. They were stranded in open water, approximately twelve miles from the shore, with no radio and no one nearby to help. After drifting for hours under the punishing tropical sun, Michael made a fateful decision. According to René (who was rescued while floating in the Arafura Sea), Michael looked toward the distant coastline and said, "I think I can make it." Then he stripped down, slipped into the water, and began swimming—alone. It was the last time anyone would ever see him alive.

His disappearance launched one of the most extensive missing persons searches of the twentieth century. Because of the Rockefeller name, no expense was spared. The family's immense wealth and political influence mobilized an international response. Helicopters, naval ships, and aircraft were deployed to comb the island and surrounding seas. Even Nelson Rockefeller and his wife flew to Dutch New Guinea, desperate to find their son. For nine days, the search pushed through the dense jungles, coastal mangroves, and shark-infested waters—but there was no trace of Michael. Not a body. Not a scrap of clothing. Nothing.

Eventually, the Dutch interior minister declared Michael Rockefeller dead, and the official cause was ruled as drowning—but rumors immediately began to spread. Some speculated that Michael had been attacked by sharks while swimming. Others imagined him still alive, having abandoned his privileged life to disappear into the jungle, finally freed from the weight of his last name. But in the villages closest to Otsjanep, whispers suggested something much darker. Some Asmat people claimed Michael had made it to shore—only to be killed. The Dutch colonial authorities strongly denied any such rumors, insisting that their investigations turned up no credible evidence.

Decades later, Carl Hoffman, a journalist and author working for *National Geographic*, reopened the cold case and spent years researching its history. In 2014, he published his findings in the explosive book *Savage Harvest*, which included a trove of overlooked evidence suggesting that Michael had, in fact, reached shore—and was killed by the Asmat.

When Carl Hoffman traveled to Otsjanep, he posed as a journalist interested in Asmat culture. With an interpreter, he interviewed local villagers and overheard a telling exchange. One elder warned another not to speak about "the American who died here." When pressed further, the elder whispered a name: Michael Rockefeller. Hoffman also discovered that two Dutch missionaries, who had lived among the Asmat for years and spoke their language fluently, had relayed disturbing accounts to the Dutch government. According to them, local Asmat warriors confessed to killing a white man who swam to shore in 1961. The story had been passed down orally through the tribe for years.

In 1962, a Dutch police officer, Wim van de Waal, was sent to investigate. He interviewed villagers and even recovered a skull said to belong to Michael. Wim concluded that the Asmat had ritually killed and cannibalized Michael—a killing they claimed was revenge for a deadly conflict in 1957, in which Dutch officials shot and killed several Asmat men. But this conclusion was buried, suppressed by Dutch colonial authorities who feared an international scandal would erupt if word got out that one of the most famous young Americans had been killed by a tribe under their watch.

According to Carl Hoffman, when Michael Rockefeller swam toward the shores of Otsjanep in 1961, he was likely exhausted, dehydrated, and desperate for help—and he was unknowingly approaching the epicenter of long-standing tribal grief. At first, the men watching from the shore mistook him for a crocodile. But as he drew nearer, they realized he was a foreigner, just like the Dutch who had killed their fathers. Unbeknownst to Michael, the group who spotted him included the sons of the Asmat men who had been killed four years earlier. And to them, Michael wasn't an innocent outsider—he was a symbol of their loss, the physical embodiment of the colonial powers that had violated their people.

Hoffman explained that, as Michael reached land, the group speared him to death on the spot. Then they decapitated him, split open his skull, and consumed his brain. His flesh was cooked and eaten, part of a spiritual ceremony meant to absorb the power of the enemy. His thigh bones were carved into daggers, and his tibias sharpened into spear tips for fishing. His blood was drained and used to anoint the tribe during a ritual dance. But the act, once complete, brought more fear than satisfaction.

Soon after Michael's disappearance, the Asmat saw something that terrified them—planes, helicopters, and boats swarming the skies and shores. The search operation for Michael was unlike anything villagers had ever seen before. And then, not long after the killing, the region was struck by a devastating cholera outbreak. Many of the villagers believed it to be a curse—divine retribution for the murder of the man who had come from across the sea.

Despite the oral accounts passed down through generations, no one ever publicly confessed to the killing. When Carl Hoffman pressed villagers for the truth, many simply said it was a story they had heard before—a tragic tale buried in communal memory, too dangerous or sacred to speak of directly.

Today, the Rockefeller collection of artifacts from Africa, Oceania, and the Americas remains on display. Though the Museum of Primitive Art was closed several years after Michael's disappearance, its collection was transferred to the Metropolitan Museum of Art, also in New York City. In 1982, the Michael C. Rockefeller Wing was built to house the collection, and, in 2025, the entire wing was renovated and reopened with a public festival. The Asmat bisj poles acquired by Michael on his expeditions are a central feature of the collection.

RESOURCES

For extra true crime, ghost stories, alien stories, and more, feel free to check out the following resources:

The website Listverse is endlessly fascinating and often disturbing. Listverse is packed with top ten lists covering the weirdest, darkest, and most mind-blowing topics on the internet. Find them at listverse.com.

The *Morbid* podcast, hosted by Alaina Urquhart and Ash Kelley. This hit podcast on Wondery covers disturbing criminal cases, creepy history, and all things strange and spooky—with storytelling that's both chilling and addictively entertaining. Listen to this wherever you get your podcasts.

Ranker is a unique website that has stories about every topic. It even lets readers vote on the stories and boost them up in the ranks. I find myself visiting this website quite often and I imagine you will, too. Visit at ranker.com.

The ScaryforKids website is a treasure trove of ghost stories, alien encounters, urban legends, and real-life horror—all organized by genre for easy browsing. Perfect for fans of the strange and supernatural. Visit at scaryforkids.com.

The True Crime Museum in the United Kingdom gives you a look into the world of serial killers and much more. This is said to be one of the best true crime museums in the world. Learn more at truecrimemuseum.co.uk.

REFERENCES

"America's Most Haunted Hospitals and Asylums." US Ghost Adventures, March 2, 2022. usghostadventures.com/haunted-places/americas-most-haunted-hospitals-and-asylums/old-tooele-hospital.

Aries, Skylar. "The Strange Disappearance of 'Shelby's Sweetheart' Asha Degree." Cold Case Explorations, April 6, 2025. coldcaseexplorations.com/north-carolina-cold-or-unsolved-cases/the-strange-disappearance-of-shelbys-sweetheart-asha-degree.

Baker, Ron. "Full Story of Nikki Catsouras Death & 'Porsche Girl' Leaked Death Photos." Mythgyaan, March 10, 2024. mythgyaan.com/nikki-catsouras.

Banks, Anthony. "The Frog Boys of South Korea." Criminally Intrigued, January 6, 2019. criminallyintrigued.com/blog/2019/1/6/the-curious-case-of-the-frog-boys.

"'Betty and Barney Hill, the New Hampshire Couple Behind One of the Most Famous 'Alien Abuctions' of All Time." All Thats Interesting. February 17, 2025. allthatsinteresting.com/betty-and-barney-hill.

"Black Hope Curse." *Unsolved Mysteries*, September 4, 2020. unsolved.com/gallery/black-hope-curse.

"Black Monk House—Everything You Need to Know About It." Strange Strange Strange, September 17, 2016. strangestrangestrange.com/paranormal/black-monk-house.

Brown, Zach. "Guy Disappears on His Way to His Daughter's Birth, Family Finds His Decapitated Body in Their Barn 6 Months Later." Oola, August 17, 2022. oola.com/social/guy-disappears-on-his-way-to-his-daughters-birth-family-finds-his-decapitated-body-in-their-barn-6-months-later.

Carter, Jake. "The Bizarre Case of the Beck Poltergeist in Indianapolis." Anomalien.com, May 29, 2020. anomalien.com/the-bizarre-case-of-the-beck-poltergeist-in-indianapolis.

Carter, Jake. "The Demons of Haunted Tooele Hospital." Anomalien.com, August 12, 2020. anomalien.com/the-demons-of-haunted-tooele-hospital.

Carter, Jake. "A Haunting in Humpty Doo: Australian Poltergeist Story." Anomalien.com, October 17, 2018. anomalien.com/a-haunting-in-humpty-doo-australian-poltergeist-story.

Carter, Jake. "The Jaboticabal Poltergeist." Anomalien.com, September 18, 2018. anomalien.com/the-jaboticabal-poltergeist.

Carter, Jake. "Mississippi Town Commemorates Historic UFO Abduction." Anomalien.com, July 19, 2022. anomalien.com/mississippi-town-commemorates-historic-ufo-abduction.

Carter, Jake. "Mysterious Zimbabwe UFO Incident." Anomalien.com, August 16, 2019. anomalien.com/mysterious-zimbabwe-ufo-incident.

Carter, Jake. "The 1969 Berkshire UFO Incident That Left a Town in Shock." Anomalien.com, December 4, 2024. anomalien.com/the-1969-berkshire-ufo-incident-that-left-a-town-in-shock.

Carter, Jake. "Pascagoula Abduction: The Lives of Two Men Turned Upside Down." Anomalien.com, January 19, 2021. anomalien.com/pascagoula-abduction.

Carter, Jake. "200 Demons House: Ammons Haunting Case." Anomalien.com, September 24, 2018. anomalien.com/200-demons-house-ammons-haunting-case.

Carter, Jake. "The Vallecas Case: The Mysterious Death of Estefania Gutierrez." Anomalien.com, August 12, 2020. anomalien.com/the-vallecas-case-the-mysterious-death-of-estefania-gutierrez.

Carter, Jake. "Was Betty and Barney Hill Abduction an MK-Ultra Test?" Anomalien.com, March 18, 2023. anomalien.com/was-betty-and-barney-hill-abduction-an-mk-ultra-test.

Chalker, Bill. "1988, DNA Sample from Khoury Abduction Raises Big Questions." DNA Sample from Abduction Case Raises Big Questions. Accessed May 12, 2025. ufocasebook.com/khouryabduction.html.

Chao, Jeffrey. "Mental Illness or Demonic Possession: Anneliese Michel." Medium, September 20, 2022. medium.com/lessons-from-history/mental-illness-or-demonic-possession-anneliese-michel-53c4a474e7d1.

Cieslik, Emma. 2024. "Death as a Child: The Modern Legend of the Black-Eyed Children." Atlas Obscura, October 16. Accessed October 7, 2025. atlasobscura.com/articles/black-eyed-children-urban-legend.

Daly, Helen. "Inside Berkshires UFO Sightings Where One Night Changed Four Families' Lives—*Unsolved Mysteries* Investigates." Radio Times, July 7, 2020. radiotimes.com/tv/documentaries/true-crime/unsolved-mysteries-berkshires-ufo-sightings-netflix-true-story.

de Sturler, Alice. "Remembering the Frog Boys." Defrosting Cold Cases, March 1, 2017. defrostingcoldcases.com/remembering-the-frog-boys.

DeLong, William. "Why 12-Year-Old Shanda Sharer Was Brutally Tortured and Killed by Four Teenage Girls." All That's Interesting, April 16, 2024. allthatsinteresting.com/shanda-sharer.

Dimuro, Gina. "Iowa Paperboy Johnny Gosch Vanished in 1982—Then the Chilling Sightings of Him Began." All That's Interesting, June 2, 2023. allthatsinteresting.com/johnny-gosch.

Elshazly, Reem. "Disturbing Miyazawa Family Murders Unsolved for over 20 Years." HubPages, 2024. discover.hubpages.com/politics/the-disturbing-setagaya-murders-the-unsolved-family-murders-that-baffled-japan-for-over-20-years.

Ewing, Jody, and Aaron Brilbeck. "Johnny Gosch." Iowa Cold Cases, January 29, 2022. iowacoldcases.org/case-summaries/johnny-gosch.

Fecou, Louie. "Maycon Roque Murder—Where Is Karina Roque Now?" Ready Steady Cut, September 18, 2024. readysteadycut.com/2023/10/05/maycon-roque-murder-karina-roque.

Forgie, Adam. "Timeline: What We Know in the Years since Susan Cox Powell Went Missing." KUTV, December 7, 2020. kutv.com/news/local/timeline-what-we-know-in-the-10-years-since-susan-cox-powell-went-missing.

Gallagher, Kona. "The Mysterious Disappearance of Ben McDaniel: A Dive into the Depths of the Unknown." *And Then They Were Gone*, December 27, 2023. andthentheyweregone.com/blog/the-mysterious-disappearance-of-ben-mcdaniel-a-dive-into-the-depths-of-the-unknown.

Gallagher, Kona. "Vanishing Act: The Story of Asha Degree's Disappearance." *And Then They Were Gone*, October 16, 2023. andthentheyweregone.com/blog/vanishing-act-the-story-of-asha-degrees-disappearance.

Giacomazzo, Bernadette. "The Chilling Story of Teresita Basa, the Woman Whose 'Ghost' May Have Solved Her Own Murder." All That's Interesting, February 27, 2024. allthatsinteresting.com/teresita-basa.

Gold, Simon. "Mystery or Tragedy: The Frederick Valentich Disappearance." Discovery UK, December 16, 2024. discoveryuk.com/mysteries/mystery-or-tragedy-the-frederick-valentich-disappearance/#:~:text=The%20disappearance%20of%20Frederick%20Valentich%2C%20a%20young%20pilot,abduction%20case%20in%20history%2C%20but%20what%20really%20happened%3F.

Goldfarb, Kara. "The Horrifying Story of Colleen Stan - 'The Girl in the Box.'" All That's Interesting, July 19, 2024. allthatsinteresting.com/girl-in-the-box-colleen-stan.

Guiley, Rosemary Ellen. "The Jaboticabal Poltergeist." Light Force Network, August 21, 2023. lightforcenetwork.com/paranorman/jaboticabal-poltergeist.

Harvey, Austin. "The Ariel Phenomenon, When Dozens of Schoolchildren in Zimbabwe Claimed They Met Aliens." All That's Interesting, October 10, 2024. allthatsinteresting.com/ariel-school-phenomenon.

Harvey, Austin. "Inside the Varginha UFO Incident, When Multiple People Reported Witnessing Extraterrestrial Phenomena in Brazil." All That's Interesting, September 13, 2024. allthatsinteresting.com/varginha-ufo-incident.

Harvey, Austin. "The Tragic Story of Nikki Catsouras' Death and the Leaked Photos of Her Grisly Car Crash." All That's Interesting, August 8, 2023. allthatsinteresting.com/nikki-catsouras-death.

"The Hauntings of the Old Tooele Hospital." Accessed May 12, 2025. haunted-places-to-go.com/old-tooele-hospital.html.

Hendley, Shona. "In 1991 Five Boys Went Searching for Frogs. Their Bodies Were Discovered 11 Years Later." Mamamia, August 26, 2019. mamamia.com.au/frog-boys.

Hintz, Charlie. "Inside the Haunted Tallmann House: Photos from the 1988 Case of a Haunted Bunk Bed in Horicon, WI." Cult of Weird, January 11, 2023. cultofweird.com/paranormal/tallmann-house-photos.

Hintz, Charlie. "The Tallman Family and the Haunted Bunk Bed in Horicon, Wisconsin." Cult of Weird, February 22, 2021. cultofweird.com/paranormal/haunted-bunk-beds-in-wisconsin.

Hoffman, Carl. "What Really Happened to Michael Rockefeller." Smithsonian.com, March 1, 2014. smithsonianmag.com/history/What-Really-Happened-to-Michael-Rockefeller-180949813.

Ishak, Natasha. "Inside the 1969 Berkshire UFO Incident That Shook a Small Massachusetts Town." All That's Interesting, October 22, 2022. allthatsinteresting.com/1969-berkshires-ufo.

Janes, DeAnna. "Nightmare on Chase Street: The Smurl Family Haunting." The Lineup, May 25, 2016. the-line-up.com/smurl-family-haunting.

K22, Sebastian. "One of the Most Disturbing Cases Ever." TikTok, 2024. tiktok.com/@sebastiank22/video/7363392441426169131?lang=en.

Kelly, Erin. "The Incredible Story of Jayme Closs and her Daring Escape from Her Kidnapper." All That's Interesting, November 13, 2024. allthatsinteresting.com/jayme-closs.

Kelly, Erin. "The Story of Kyron Horman, the 7-Year-Old Whose Disappearance Spawned the Largest Manhunt in Oregon History." All That's Interesting, February 27, 2024. allthatsinteresting.com/kyron-horman.

Kuroski, John. "Lost in the Ashes: The Mystery of the Vanished Sodder Children." All That's Interesting, December 13, 2024. allthatsinteresting.com/sodder-children.

"Kyron Richard Horman." The Charley Project. Accessed May 12, 2025. charleyproject.org/case/kyron-richard-horman.

Leigh, Natasha. "The Unsolved Disappearance of Brian Shaffer." Medium, March 23, 2024. medium.com/@natasha.leigh/the-unsolved-disappearance-of-brian-shaffer-fbcdb92a1338.

Liles, Jordan. "Frederick Valentich's 'UFO' Sighting and Disappearance." Snopes, November 18, 2024. www.snopes.com/articles/383824/frederick-valentich-ufo-disappearance.

Liv. "Murder by Neglect—the Deaths of Lacey Fletcher and Valerie Wallach." True Crime Society, May 22, 2022. truecrimesocietyblog.com/2022/05/22/murder-by-neglect-the-death-of-lacey-fletcher.

Lowth, Marcus. "The Haunting of East Drive and the Black Monk of Pontefract." UFO Insight, October 4, 2021. ufoinsight.com/supernatural/ghosts-hauntings/east-drive-black-monk-pontefract.

Lynch, CJ. "The Haunted: Skirvin Hotel." The Morbid Library, December 10, 2020. themorbidlibrary.com/the-haunted-skirvin-hotel.

Lyon, Rivy. "Inside the Horrific Murder of Tim McLean Aboard a Greyhound Bus in 2008." All That's Interesting, August 7, 2024. allthatsinteresting.com/tim-mclean.

Macrae, Meghan. "The Horrific Case of Anneliese Michel's Possession and Exorcism." CVLT Nation, November 17, 2022. cvltnation.com/horrific-case-anneliese-michels-possession-excorcism.

Margaritoff, Marco. "The Disturbing Disappearance of Susan Powell, the Utah Mother Presumed Murdered by Her Husband." All That's Interesting, April 22, 2024. allthatsinteresting.com/susan-powell.

Margaritoff, Marco. "Inside the Mysterious Disappearance of Brian Shaffer, the Medical Student Who Vanished from an Ohio Bar." All That's Interesting, October 30, 2023. allthatsinteresting.com/brian-shaffer.

Margaritoff, Marco. "The 9 Most Convincing Alien Abduction Stories in Modern History." All That's Interesting, January 9, 2025. allthatsinteresting.com/alien-abductions/4.

Margaritoff, Marco. "The Story of Asha Degree, the 9-Year-Old Girl Who Mysteriously Vanished in 2000." All That's Interesting, July 9, 2024. allthatsinteresting.com/asha-degree.

Mehrotra, Kriti. "Susan Powell's Disappearance: What Happened to Her? Has She Been Found?" The Cinemaholic, July 25, 2024. thecinemaholic.com/susan-powell-disappearance.

Meisfjord, Tom. "The Truth behind the Exorcism of Michael Taylor." Grunge, July 20, 2020. grunge.com/228121/the-truth-behind-the-exorcism-of-michael-taylor.

The Michael C. Rockefeller Wing. The Metropolitan Museum of Art. Accessed July 23, 2025. metmuseum.org/hubs/the-michael-c-rockefeller-wing.

Mitchell, Dawn. "The 1965 Torture and Murder of Sylvia Likens." *The Indianapolis Star*, December 3, 2019. indystar.com/story/news/history/retroindy/2013/10/24/sylvia-likens/3178393.

Moran, Frank. "The Black Monk of Pontefract (1966): Unveiling the True Horror Story That Still Haunts West Yorkshire." Horror Galore, March 4, 2024. horrorgalore.com/true-story/title-black-monk-pontefract-1966-unveiling-true-horror-story-still-haunts-west-yorkshire.

Moran, Frank. "The True Story of the Perron Family—Page 2." Horror Galore, January 12, 2016. horrorgalore.com/true-story/next-pages/true-story-perron-family-page-2.

Morgan, Amber. "Latoya Ammons, the Woman Who Allegedly Battled 200 Spirits Inside the 'Demon House' of Gary, Indiana." All That's Interesting, March 25, 2025. allthatsinteresting .com/latoya-ammons.

Morgan, Amber. "The True Story of the Terrifying Events Behind 'The Haunting in Connecticut.'" All That's Interesting, October 31, 2024. allthatsinteresting.com/haunting-in -connecticut-true-story.

Morgan, Kate. "A Christmas Eve Mystery: What Happened to the Sodder Children?" HowStuffWorks, February 16, 2023. people.howstuffworks.com/sodder-children.htm.

"The Mysterious Death of Mateusz Kawecki: A Journey That Ended in Tragedy." Talk to Learn, October 21, 2024. talktolearnesl.com/the-mysterious-death-of-mateusz-kawecki-a -journey-that-ended-in-tragedy.

Navarro, Hector. "The Haunted Tallman House of Horicon, Wisconsin." Factschology, January 14, 2023. factschology.com/mmm-podcast-articles/haunted-tallman-house-horicon -wisconsin.

Newkirk, Greg. "Long Haul Trucker Shares Harrowing Experience of Wife's Alien Abduction, Suicide." Sott.net, 2013. sott.net/article/256565-Long-haul-trucker-shares-harrowing -experience-of-wifes-alien-abduction-suicide.

Nicewanger, Steve. "The Indianapolis Poltergeist." *The Weekly View*. Accessed May 12, 2025. weeklyview.net/2015/10/29/the-indianapolis-poltergeist.

Paoletti, Gabe. "The Story of Michael Rockefeller's Disappearance and the Gruesome Theories Behind It." All That's Interesting, August 30, 2024. allthatsinteresting.com/michael -rockefeller.

Paulo, Derrick A. "Intrigue, Scandal, Heartbreak: The Case of South Korea's Missing 'Frog Boys.'" CNA. Accessed May 12, 2025. channelnewsasia.com/cnainsider/intrigue-scandal -heartbreak-case-south-korea-missing-frog-boys-774406.

Pearl, Diana. "How Did a Second-Grader in Oregon Seemingly Vanish from His School in 2010—and Who Is Responsible?" *People*, September 13, 2017. people.com/crime/kyron -horman-disappearance-timeline.

"The Puzzling Death of Mateusz Kawecki in Poland." StrangeOutdoors.com, September 2024. strangeoutdoors.com/strange-indoors/mateusz-kawecki.

Quackenbush, Thomm. "The True Story of the Disappearance of the Sodder Children." Grunge, April 8, 2021. grunge.com/377440/the-true-story-of-the-disappearance-of-the-sodder-children.

Redd, Wyatt. "Inside the Myrtles Planation and the Story of Its Haunting." All That's Interesting, June 17, 2024. allthatsinteresting.com/myrtles-plantation.

Rowton, Erik. "The Haunting of the Perron Family: The 'True' Story behind the *Conjuring* Movie." The Paranormal Scholar, June 2, 2017. paranormalscholar.com/perron-family-haunting.

Rowton, Erik. "The Vallecas Case: The Haunting True Story behind Netflix Horror Movie 'Veronica.'" The Paranormal Scholar, April 27, 2018. paranormalscholar.com/el-caso-vallecas.

Serena, Katie. "The Gruesome True Story of the Unsolved Hinterkaifeck Murders." All That's Interesting, October 20, 2023. allthatsinteresting.com/hinterkaifeck-murders.

Serena, Katie. "The Horrific Crimes of Vince Li, the Man Who Killed and Cannibalized Tim McLean on a Greyhound Bus in 2008." All That's Interesting, April 21, 2025. allthatsinteresting.com/vince-li.

Serena, Katie. "Inside the Unexplained Disappearance of Frederick Valentich." All That's Interesting, April 16, 2022. allthatsinteresting.com/frederick-valentich.

Serena, Katie. "The True Story of *The Conjuring*: The Perron Family and Enfield Haunting." All That's Interesting, February 12, 2025. allthatsinteresting.com/true-story-of-the-conjuring-perron-family-enfield-haunting.

Short, Michelle. "The Bizarre Disappearance of Brian Shaffer." HubPages. Accessed May 12, 2025. discover.hubpages.com/politics/The-Bizarre-Disappearance-of-Brian-Shaffer.

Shreya, Kumari. "Ben McDaniel: What Happened to Him? Has He Been Found?" The Cinemaholic, March 8, 2024. thecinemaholic.com/ben-mcdaniel-disappeared.

Slater, Anna. "Girl Tortures Brother, 5, to Death and Eats His Penis during 'Satanic Ritual.'" *Daily Mirror*, April 8, 2019. mirror.co.uk/news/uk-news/cannibal-girl-tortures-brother-5-14252395.

"The Smurl Poltergeist." Accessed May 12, 2025. thecobrasnose.com/xxghost/smurl.html.

"The Snedeker House Haunting: Real Poltergeist or Hoax?" Hauntingrealm. Accessed May 12, 2025. hauntingrealm.com/snedeker-house-haunting.

Stockton, Chrissy. "16 Terrifying Encounters with 'the Black Eyed Kids.'" Thought Catalog, January 16, 2024. thoughtcatalog.com/christine-stockton/2013/11/16-peoples-terrifying-encounters-with-the-black-eyed-kids.

"The Story of Anneliese Michel." *A True Crime Podcast*, March 21, 2025. crimeandcoffeecouple.com/2025/01/07/the-story-of-anneliese-michel.

"The Strange Case of Dr. Herbert Hopkins." UFO Casebook News. Accessed May 12, 2025. ufocasebook.com/2014/strange-case-of-dr-hopkins.html#:~:text=Hopkins,%20a%20doctor%20and%20hypnotist,%20was%20hired%20as,be%20from%20the%20New%20Jersey%20UFO%20Research%20Organisation.

Sumter, Angelica N. "Allan Showery: The Tragic Murder of Teresita Basa and the 'Voice' That May Have Helped Solve Her Case." Daily Crime, February 23, 2023. dailycrime.com/allan-showery-the-tragic-murder-of-teresita-basa-and-the-voice-that-may-have-helped-solve-her-case.

Sutherland, Paul. "The Ossett 'Exorcist' Murder." The True Crime Enthusiast, February 3, 2022. thetruecrimeenthusiast.co.uk/the-ossett-exorcist-murder.

"Sylvia Likens and 'Indiana's Most Terrible Crime,'" Sylvia's Child Advocacy Center. Accessed October 7, 2025. sylviascac.org/sylvias-story.

Taylor, Troy. "The Bizarre Case Of The Beck Poltergeist In Indianapolis." Paranormal.lt, May 31, 2020. Accessed October 7, 2025. paranormal.lt/the-bizarre-case-of-the-beck-poltergeist-in-indianapolis.

Taylor, Troy. "Myrtles Plantation Legends, Lore and Lies." American Hauntings. Accessed May 12, 2025. americanhauntingsink.com/myrtles.

Thompson, Emily G. "The Halloween Beheading Murder of Patricia Ward" Morbidology, February 24, 2022. morbidology.com/the-halloween-beheading-murder-of-patricia-ward.

Tinning, Danielle. "Inside the Grisly Case of Cassie Jo Stoddart, the Teenage Girl Killed by Her Classmates – for Fun." All That's Interesting, August 8, 2024. allthatsinteresting.com/cassie-jo-stoddart.

"The Torture and Murder of Sylvia Likens." True Crime Edition, June 5, 2022. truecrimeedition.com/post/sylvia-likens.

Vanapalli, Viswa. "Cassie Stoddart Murder: Where Are Brian Draper and Torey Adamcik Now?" The Cinemaholic, June 10, 2022. thecinemaholic.com/cassie-jo-stoddart-murder-where-are-brian-draper-and-torey-adamcik-now.

Vanapalli, Viswa. "Shanda Sharer Murder: Where Are Her Killers Now?" The Cinemaholic, August 19, 2022. thecinemaholic.com/shanda-sharer-murder-where-are-her-killers-now.

"The Varginha Incident: Unraveling the Mystery of Brazil's Roswell." The Paranormal Playground Podcast, November 14, 2024. theparanormalplayground.co/the-varginha-incident.

Vatomsky, Sonya. "The Chilling Story of the Hinterkaifeck Killings, Germany's Most Famous Unsolved Crime." Mental Floss, July 24, 2023. mentalfloss.com/article/502044/chilling-story-hinterkaifeck-killings-germanys-most-famous-unsolved-crime.

Verma, Vicky. "Peter Khoury Abduction: Mystery of Blonde Alien Woman Hair Found on His Body in 1992." How and Why's, March 19, 2024. howandwhys.com/peter-khoury-alien-abduction-case.

Wehrstein, KM. "Pollock Twins (Reincarnation Case)." Psi Encyclopedia, 2017. psi-encyclopedia.spr.ac.uk/articles/pollock-twins-reincarnation-case.

White, Caleb. "Mystery of the Pollock Sisters: Is It Possible to Have Twins without a Family History of Them?" Science Times, June 19, 2024. sciencetimes.com/articles/50790/20240619/mystery-pollock-sisters-possible-twins-without-family-history.htm.

Wiki, Contributors to Unsolved Mysteries. "Black Hope." *Unsolved Mysteries* Wiki. Accessed May 12, 2025. unsolvedmysteries.fandom.com/wiki/Black_Hope.

Zed, Ellie. "Reincarnation: Are the Pollock Twins Proof of Rebirth or a Hoax?" Paranorms, October 28, 2021. paranorms.com/pollock-twins.

Zoey. "The Real Haunting Story of the Connecticut Snedeker's House." Hub Pages. Accessed May 12, 2025. discover.hubpages.com/religion-philosophy/The-Real-Haunting-In-Connecticut.

ABOUT THE AUTHOR

SEBASTIAN KRAHL is a renowned content creator from Pennsylvania, with over 9.5 million followers across TikTok, YouTube, Facebook, and Snapchat. Known for his chilling deep dives into true crime, paranormal encounters, and unexplained mysteries, Sebastian has captivated a global audience with billions of views on his videos. His journey as a content creator began at just thirteen years old, though he briefly stepped away to pursue sports during his teenage years. In 2019, at the age of nineteen, Sebastian returned to content creation with a renewed focus—this time on the dark and disturbing stories that many shy away from. Through daily uploads and relentless dedication, he built a loyal following and became a leading voice in the world of horror and true crime storytelling. You can find his content under the handle **Sebastiank22**. This is Sebastian's debut book.

ABOUT THE ILLUSTRATOR

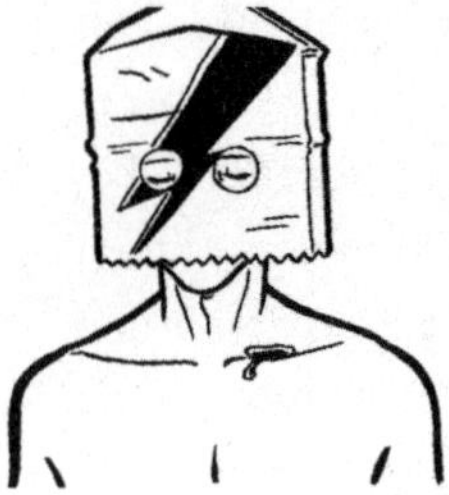

FÁBIO LYRA is an illustrator and an award-winning cartoonist. He is the author of the comics *Menina Infinito*, *Clube do Single*, and *Stoned Teenagers from Outer Space*, and he has contributed to several other comic books, magazines, and anthologies. As an illustrator, he creates gig posters, flyers, and album art for underground bands and works in both advertising and publishing, illustrating magazines, books, and more.